The Greatest BANKING SCANDAL in History

And How It Affects You

Keep

DOUG CLARK

Federal Reserve p. 25-33

Harvest House Publishers
Eugene, Oregon 97402

**Dedicated to
Former Congressman Wright Patman of Texas
Chairman of the Committee
on Banking and Currency**

For more than 40 years Congressman Wright Patman studied, worked, and labored to preserve for the American people a proper money-supply and interest-rate system via the Federal Reserve System.

No one has understood banking and all its vast ramifications for this nation better than Congressman Wright Patman. No man tried harder to change the seemingly incorrigible situation for the American people than Congressman Patman.

He wrote a 145-page presentation to the 88th Congress on money. It is the greatest in existence and was presented to the Committee on Banking and Currency, House of Representatives, on August 5, 1964, with the purpose of changing the current system of interest rates and money-supply regulation.

Since then things have gone from bad to worse and from worse to evil. The depression he envisioned is upon us, for the reasons Mr. Patman cited.

His book seems to have been lost in congressional files and in the U.S. Government Printing Office in Washington, D.C. But it was not lost—it was suppressed and stifled. Out of the one copy I have, sent to me by an interested friend, I present to you the material I have gathered from Washington, from across the nation, and especially from Congressman Wright Patman, without whose work this book would not be possible. He died attempting to free this nation of its monetary yoke and heaviest curse. May his life and death not be in vain.

Contents

Preface

Shocking economic statistics confront us every month. By the time the month has finished we are all well aware of this as we live in our warped world of money, purchasing power, consumer goods, and deteriorating standard of living.

Mr. Average American Worker gets his semiannual raises in pay. His benefits have not disappeared as far as medical and insurance care are concerned, but he is buying less and enjoying less of American and foreign-made goods. His family, though spending more dollars, is receiving far less in value during this decade of the eighties than they did in the sixties or even in the seventies. *Why?*

Our average wage-earner reads about *inflation* every day in the paper, hears about it on the radio, and watches the statistics pile up on the TV news in the evening. After 200 years of great growth and marvelous productivity in the United States and Canada, why does the standard of living now have to shrink, shrivel, and diminish?

What went wrong with the private-enterprise system? Did the government all of a sudden make unexplainable errors that have led to this situation in which the dollar is dying?

Has the free-enterprise system run its course? Was it only a dream based on unreality? Could it have been a bubble bound to burst eventually because it was started on a false premise?

Was there a curse from the beginning on this lovely way of life that was eating away our innards from the commencement of the private-enterprise system?

What did we miss?

Where did we fail?

Who overlooked what?

It was working so grandly in every way. Immigrants would give their souls to come to this land from their homelands in order to start from a shoestring and become prosperous.

And millions of them made it just that way. They came from Italy and opened fruit and vegetable stands. Their first-generation children went to universities and made their immigrant parents so proud. The system of free and private enterprise did this for them.

Greeks came and plunged into the restaurant business, and made Americans from every land feel the impact of their culinary genius while they built homes, established themselves with financial solvency, and helped America be what it is today.

On came the Irish—at first hated, but they made it to the top. The English wanted this land for themselves, but their free men escaped the bondage of taxes, the forced religious decrees, and the cruel and unnecessary punishments for going their private way. So they shipped themselves with little more than they had on their backs to the "land of the free."

The Germans came with their farming ideas and technological propensities and helped build farming communities and steel mills.

The French brought their latest culinary arts as well as artisans of all kinds and finally led us in the fashion industry of New York and Toronto.

The Dutch, the Swedes, the Danes, and the Norwegians—all came by the thousands, along with Asiatics and Orientals and Blacks, each from their remote sections of the blighted world. They came with hope, thrills, anticipations, and dreams of wealth, happiness, and peace. They came to be free from governments that oppressed them and from systems and traditions that bound them forever to drudgery and poverty.

Then came the Jews, with their unusual ability to do anything at all. They had been "chosen in the beginning" to give the nations the Word of God—the Bible. It appears that over the centuries God gave them the ability to do anything that needed to be done or could be done in industry, commerce, and entertainment.

America was the land of the free and home of the brave. If you were brave enough to start a business and people wanted what you made, produced, or sold, you had it made. The free-enterprise system meant that you could start without government intervention. You could grow as large as you wanted to. All you needed was intestinal fortitude (guts) and a knowledge of what you wanted to do, and you had the authority to do it. The fact that many others wanted to do the same thing only made you more competitive, thoughtful, and diligently shrewd in order to survive. Competition was not a curse—it was a creator of genius, innovation, and better goods and services for all to enjoy. Challenge to that early businessman meant that he worked harder, made a better product, or provided a better, finer, more sensitive service to his customers, and thus made more money and became prosperous.

The biggest problems of the early Americans and Canadians were competition, physical hardships, lack of money to get started, or lack of development of the nations.

It is entirely different today. Originally the private-enterprise system was encouraged by the government and financed by a controlled banking system, with adequate funds for every businessman who could prove that he had a worthwhile idea. He could borrow the money at a very low and reasonable interest rate, and develop and grow in business.

What makes it so hard to stay in business today? Lack of money to get started and lack of money to continue. Why? High interest rates imposed on the nation by the Federal Reserve System of the United States.

The key to the origin of the twin countries of North America was available talent from overseas, available money to work and build with, and free land from a government that encouraged you to get to work and get the job done.

The key to today's lack of unemployment and business bankruptcies is the interference of government in business (with regulations that stifle initiative) and the lack of available money for private enterprise.

What has happened?

This book will detail what has happened and is happening now.

The facts will explain not only *what* has happened but *why*, and where we are going from here.

But even more important, this book can tell you *what to do* to save yourself and your family from disaster.

I firmly believe that as you are armed with the knowledge of the hidden facts about your money, *you will know what to do to save your equities, savings, fortunes, and lives in the oncoming onslaught of fortunes, lives, and families.*

Through it all, my prayer is that you will not only survive with your family, but that you will prosper and be successful with God's help.

1

The Amazing Facts

Virtually all bankers, senators, and members of the public in business are being brainwashed into believing that the highest prime interest rate ever imposed on the American public is necessary in order to "cut inflation." Nothing could be further from the truth.

Inflation has not been altered by the astronomically high prime interest rate as set by the multinational bankers of the United States. As a matter of fact, at the same time that we have had the highest money supply in the nation's history, we have also suffered the tragedy of the highest interest rates in history. The latter are supposed to militate against the former, but high interest rates have not affected the money supply-inflation problems one bit!

But we do know that over 600,000 businesses went out of business in 1980 because of the high interest rates. Almost 400,000 went bankrupt and the rest just closed the door.

High interest rates do not affect the influx and increase of inflation. The Federal Reserve System has been creating cash and credit money at the greatest rate ever, while businesses have been plunging into recessions and bankruptcies, and initiative has been stifled at an unprecedented rate, exceeded only in 1929!

High interest rates have created joblessness, and the unemployment lines are lengthening as the most optimistic forecast predicts much more joblessness in the 80's in spite of everything the new president and his able cabinet can do.

Why? Simply because neither the president nor his administration nor congress directly control the rate of interest known as the prime. It is set arbitrarily by the international bankers wherever and whenever they wish, with no governmental controls.

You will learn about the Feds and about the Federal Reserve System, in this book, but you will learn also about the Multinational Bankers of the eight major banks and others who set their own prime rate so that when buying government securities, (when the government needs billions of dollars to pay off its debts) they force the government into paying near the prime rate, thereby ripping off the government and raping the hard-working people of this nation of their profits.

This is the greatest transfer of wealth ever to take place in America. The money is being transferred from the hardworking producers to the nonworking, nonproductive takers and leeches of America. They have no conscience. They pledge allegiance to no country. They just love the dollar.

They manipulate the stock market overnight by knowing the rates are being raised or lowered. They buy in when stocks are low and rates are high, and they sell out when rates are lowered and stocks are high. They do the same with the commodities market for gold and silver.

Mr. President: Stop the manipulation of the prime interest rates, and save America for Americans.

It can be done.

If it isn't done, what will take place in the decade of the 80's will make 1929-33 look like a Sunday-school picnic.

Higher interest rates mean thousands more business bankruptcies and personal business failures due to the high cost of borrowing.

But this will only cut consumer demand, thereby putting the country into further recession, bordering on depression.

All the while the federal government is spending *over two billion dollars a day!* Over half of this amount will have to be created by the Fed and other bankers and parties to monetize government expenditures of approximately 800 billion dollars for 1982-83! There is where your inflation is coming from—not from consumer demand.

We are going to have a credit collapse, a currency collapse, a real estate collapse, and an incredible depression in America unless we stop this wild government spending and terminate this uncontrolled use of spiraling interest rates.

We can only stretch the elasticity of the dollar so far. It will soon snap. Depression will follow immediately. The Housing and Auto industries are predictors of what is to come. Both are suffering their worst collapse since the 1929 depression, taking many other support industries with them.

There are over 14,000 local commercial banks in the United States, and over 4500 savings and loans. In the coming three years you are going to see bankruptcies, failures, and mergers such as never before in the financial banking world. Many of these institutions will collapse because of the domino effect of the third world countries (LDC's—lesser-developed countries) not being able to pay their interest or any part of the principle on a 500-billion-dollar-debt to the U.S. banks!

Debt financing for local and state governments has risen fourfold in the past four years.

Federal-government debt increased to over one trillion dollars as President Reagan took office. The interest payment annually to monetize the federal debt is over 80 billion dollars!

The steel industry, rubber industry, and plastic industry are all suffering because of lack of demand in the auto and housing industries.

Real estate in Detroit, Chicago, and other major cities where steel, and auto production is down by over 50 percent is slipping fast and perilously. Millions of dollars in real-estate values have already been lost, and we are just seeing the beginning.

Each recession for the past 30 years has been worse than the one before it, as in each case consumer debt has been higher, consumer credit-buying deeper, government debt broader, and the inflation rate higher.

Thus each recession is getting worse, with the foregoing circumstances pushing us into a deeper depression.

The U.S. government budget is out of control. It has to grow 20 percent or more each year, without increasing benefits, just to keep up with the inflation rate. Inflation feeds on inflation, especially when you are in the billion-dollar range.

The government budget is about 40 percent of the total GNP (gross national product) of the whole nation for the early part of the 80's. This means greater inflation and less private enterprise—to a dangerous extent.

When private enterprise is down and government spending compensates, you have greater governmental control of the private enterprise system, and the final end is socialism.

Government programs of a bigger and bigger nature, while taking the place of the private sector, have to be financed either through increased taxation or inflation of the currency, and this is a killer to the nation because it results in socialization and/or depression or both.

From all available sources, I have determined that liquidity is down throughout the important sectors of the financial part of the nation—dangerously and unprecedentedly so.

Corporate liquidity is unbelievably low, as corporations borrow to the hilt, causing the greatest figures in corporate credit buying in history. Thus corporate debt is the worst ever.

Banking liquidity is the worst in human history, with banks loaning out money at the greatest rate and ratio ever known in the history of the goldsmiths and bankers. They are so illiquid and are so far into debt creation as to be one of the chief causes of inflation.

Of course the government is totally illiquid all the time. It spends much more than it takes in (in taxes), to the extent that government is the main initiator and instigator of inflation and is feeding this inflation to our trading partners the world over, causing an international imbalance monetarily and the creation of an international Western-world depression.

2

The Exciting History of Money

FACT 1—PAPER MONEY ONLY REPRESENTS REAL WEALTH: IT IS NOT WEALTH.

Paper money as you and I understand it today is the creation of international bankers in collaboration with governments of the various nations. It is a monetary concoction of the last two centuries. Prior to that time, down through the centuries, people went from simple bartering to the sophisticated computer credit money of today.

If you had a cow and I had a horse, and both of us wanted what the other man had, we could swap. Or you could swap anything for what the other man wanted to sell. It later developed into wampum, leather, metals, and then coins.

Gold and silver have the longest record of purchasing power and thus have been used as money longer than any other creation of mankind. They still have the greatest number of followers in the world, and more people in the various nations of the world look to the reality of gold and silver than to any other thing used as monetary power.

Though various governments in the last two thousand years (beginning with Rome) have tried to castigate users and holders of gold and silver and have outlawed usage of these precious metals, they still remain the only true havens of wealth known to mankind.

As gold and silver became more and more acceptable and available to the people of Europe (and also more and more difficult to manage and transport), holders of gold and silver went into business, free-enterprise style, and were the honest men who held the securities of others and kept them safe.

These early bankers then learned that they could be not only the *holders* but also the *lenders* of other people's money. They learned that less than 10 percent of the owners would come in regularly to exchange their gold and silver for other items. The early bankers soon learned that if they had a letter of agreement with the original owners, they could loan out the value of their holding to someone else, just on letters of intent, indicating that the holders did indeed have in trust the gold and silver indicated in the letters of transactions. If they loaned it out for the owners, the owners could get some small interest fee in return, but of course it developed into the banker making the lion's share because of the high interest he charged the new borrowers on the other man's money.

It soon became apparent that very little actual money had to be physically carried about from place to place for transactions. A man who wished to buy a horse or food could merely sign a note indicating that he had the money at the "holders" and that if the retailer who was selling wished to claim his new money for services or products sold, he could. In this way, paper money came into circulation, representing gold and silver held by the local banker.

The paper represented what the owner had banked, which was precious metals. These were internationally recognized for their intrinsic value and international purchasing power for any items in any country.

The new bankers found that they could not only make money by storing the precious metals for the original owners, but they could make much more money by loaning out what didn't belong to them. They became the first loan sharks.

If you can find an honest banker today, you have found a gem of character. But if you look closely you will find that most American bankers (except for local community bankers) are a crooked breed of gamblers, cheaters, and connivers who manipulate your dollars in such an unpatriotic manner and with such fervor that it is unbelievable.

FACT 2—THE HOUSE OF ROTHSCHILD WAS SET UP IN EUROPE.

It became apparent to the holders of precious metals that this was the way to go. Loan out the money, charge interest, and make money on someone else's commodity (plus the storage charge).

Meyer Amschel Rothschild of Germany discovered that secret, and, being above average in intelligence, he realized that this type of business could be exported and controlled and could become the greatest power on earth.

It was not long after these holders of money got into business that the wealthy in government—kings, princes, lords etc.—came to them for storage (as well as the average businessman).

But what about the lord who had to travel to another country? What about the ambassadors, the princes, and the heads of state, who engaged in international business and thus had expenses to engage in and think about? His local notes might not be acceptable in the other country to which he was traveling. Gold and silver in large amounts could be prohibitive to carry because of weights and robbery.

Thus Meyer conceived the idea of international banking for the Europeans and their leaders.

He set son Carl over the Bank of Naples in Italy, his son James over the Bank of France, and his son Edmund over the bank of Germany, his son Solomon over the Bank of Vienna, and his son Nathan over the Bank of England.

The Rothschild family thus controlled international banking in Europe for a long time.

Whenever a count or a prince traveled to another country, his note was now acceptable. One brother knew the writing of the other, and his signature and the international banking idea became the way of life for Europeans.

Travelers did not have to transport large amounts of gold and silver to transact business, but they could take their letters of credit from one area to another with no difficulty of recognition.

This became the acceptable means of transacting business. Governments did not coin money or make paper money. They used the holder and the bankers for their storage of gold and silver, and later the letters of credit and notes.

FACT 3—GOVERNMENTS (KINGS) NEEDED MONEY FOR WARS.

It wasn't long until one nation warring against another ran out of gold and silver from the national treasuries, or else ran precipitously short. It was then the governments learned that they too could borrow from the holders.

The bankers soon learned that to loan to the king meant big loans and thus big profits on the interest charged.

It became an overnight revelation to the Rothschild family that *the way to unfathomable riches was through financing the kings' needs in war and peace.*

But it was also instantly evident that the kings could usually finance their own needs in times of peace through heavy taxation on the people or else through business that the government might be into.

So it became expedient for the bankers to encourage wars, that they would be called upon to finance the warring governments. They sat back and watched as the British fought the French, and the Germans fought the British, and the Italians fought the other nations. Cleverly, through their national banks, they loaned each set of leaders what they needed to buy supplies and finance the terrible wars, and while the wars were going on they had family conferences on how well they were doing!

Solomon Rothschild, of the Bank of Germany, could and would confer with Nathan Rothschild of the Bank of England, on how loans and interest monies were producing family fortunes—over wine and dinner in a French restaurant far from the warring front lines.

History reveals in many books that these international bankers set up the war in the United States between the North and the South, and that this war was planned in Europe by the bankers.

France via James would finance the South and Nathan via England would finance the North.

They were prepared to finance English troops for the North and French troops to aid the South if need be.

The Czar of Russia learned of the plot and sent messages to President Lincoln stating that Russian troops would help him squash it if French troops entered the South to fight.

He knew that the war was caused by bankers for their own material gain. They used the Lincoln disparagement over the slave situation as an apparent cause for the bloodshed, but the real cause was that they wanted to split the country into two nations, to finance the split through central banks which they would shortly thereafter set up, and to continue their money-making spree with governments, kings, counts, and countries.

With the threat of Russian troops intervening, they despaired of using European soldiers and let the North and the South fight it out by themselves. Both sides were financed by the House of Rothschild Bankers of Europe, who extracted great revenues and interest from the war.

FACT 4—INTERNATIONAL BANKERS STILL FORCE WARS AND FINANCE THEM.

The books in my bibliography will furnish you details on how, when World War One broke out (with the leaders of Germany against other nations in Europe), it was the bankers that financed it, encouraged it, and made the most economically from it.

The Kaiser was a friend of the bankers and listened to their ideas of European conquest for Germany.

World War Two was encouraged by the next breed of international banker, both in North America and in Europe. They helped finance Hitler against France and England.

In America the war was encouraged by the forces behind the international bankers, who had a large hand in the affairs of the country through the Federal Reserve System, which was set up and running full swing as a private organization. (We will deal with this later as another fact of money affecting your life today.)

International bankers always stay close to the government heads at all levels. They differ drastically from the banker around the corner, where you and I bank. The bank around the corner in all probability has a good citizen running it. He probably knows nothing of what you and I are studying, and if he does know of it, he will be especially anxious for you to know that he is completely different. He may make much money for his bank locally, but he is serving his community, as banks were originally set up and intended to do.

Don't put all bankers in the same basket. Most of them on the local level are excellent and honest men, helping their community grow. Many of them do not understand how the Federal Reserve System functions. They too wonder at high interest rates and demands that are made to "pull in loans." It is amazing what local bankers do not know of international banking. But it is really not too surprising, since nobody knows everything about his business and how others deal in it.

FACT 5—INTERNATIONAL BANKERS MADE ENEMIES FOR OTHER KINGS AND USED THIS AS COLLATERAL ON THEIR LOANS.

It is common knowledge that when you and I borrow money from a bank we usually need collateral in order to borrow. (Collateral is an article or commodity that the bank can put a lien on in order to loan us the money we require.)

But how would a banker control a king or prince or politician in very high standing? Certainly there would be government property that could be used and later sued upon to gain back what was owned. But what would keep a king from simply eliminating the banker? He could arrange an accident so that there would be no banker to harass him. But bankers were clever. They set up an alien power—another king or another warring nation—that they could finance against the one they had money coming from. If he did not pay up, they would set adverse reactions against him quickly.

Bankers instigated wars to get repayment as well as interest, and they made themselves exceedingly rich in doing so. They also made themselves hated by those who did understand and by those who didn't.

These bankers learned that all men succumb to the power of money and riches. They would often buy positions of power in kings' courts (and more lately in presidents' cabinets) in order to help form policies to their personal pleasing.

There is no question in my mind that President Carter owed favors to the international bankers who helped put him into office in 1976. He repaid those political debts by bringing in men like Zbigniew Brzezinski as Secretary of National Security and Paul Volcker as head of the Federal Reserve Board. But more on these political economic facts later.

FACT 6—INTERNATIONAL BANKERS TRIED FOR YEARS TO ESTABLISH A PRIVATELY OWNED CENTRAL BANK IN THE UNITED STATES AND CANADA. THEY FAILED AND FAILED, BUT THEN COMPLETELY SUCCEEDED IN 1913.

If an international banker could succeed in loaning much money to a government through the king or prime minister, he could then exercise greater control over the policies of the regime to which he loaned the money.

It was always preferable for the bankers to have "their man" or "their men" in key positions in the king's cabinet.

In order to control George Washington, international bankers from the dawn of the United Colonies and the development of the Dominion of Canada sought to control the banking establishment.

Independently run local banks had sprung up all over the colonies and provinces originally, but the elitist bankers of Europe wanted to set up central banks for Canada and the United States—banks that they would control and thereby control the policies of the leaders through the power of loaned money and powerful positions bought by the power of loaned gold.

Presidents Lincoln and Garfield both recognized the devastating effect which these bankers had in Europe on leaders and their policies, and they feared the control they wanted so feverishly in the newly formed countries of North America.

Lincoln stated that the government could print its own money and proceeded to do so, with an excellent record of manageability.

He fought the central-bank idea and stated that it would only happen over his dead body—and it took that!

History reveals that J.P. Morgan was the chief American-born (but Germany- and England-educated) banker who represented the European interests of the bankers in the U.S. It was Morgan who allegedly precipitated banking calamities by circulating notices to call in loans, thereby creating bankruptcies and economic casualties in the U.S. and thus making the forming of a central bank seem more reasonable. He brought about the panic of 1907 and later helped in the 1913 formulation of the Federal Reserve System.

It was a German-born banker, Paul Warburg, who finally set in motion the action culminating in the legislation providing the Fed with its current powers over Americans.

He immigrated to the U.S. in 1902, leaving his family bank in Frankfurt to another brother by the name of Max, who later helped to finance the Russian Bolshevik Revolution from Germany.

The House of Rothschild was also a powerful influence in early American banking. President Jackson abolished the early effort at establishing a central bank in 1836, but even after that European Central Bankers had a long record of influencing banking procedures in the U.S.

Because of this control in Canada and the U.S., a series of panics were arranged so that the final blow to centralize would be acceptable to the leadership. Problems were created in both Canada and the United States that were used to convince bankers and the authorities that centralization was the only way to go.

Gary Allen, noted author of many best-sellers (including *None Dare Call It Conspiracy*), notes the following dealings of Paul Warburg.

Paul Warburg, born in Germany, married Nina Loeb, daughter of Solomon Loeb of Kuhn, Loeb and Company, America's most powerful international banking firm. His brother Felix married Frieda Schiff, daughter of Jacob Schiff, the ruling power behind Kuhn, Loeb & Co. In the eighteenth century the Schiffs and Rothschilds shared a double house in Frankfurt banking circles. Schiff reportedly bought his partnership in Kuhn, Loeb & Co. with Rothschild money.

Both Paul and Felix Warburg became partners in Kuhn, Loeb & Co.

In 1907, the year of the Morgan-precipitated panic in banking, Paul Warburg began spending almost all his time writing and lecturing on the need for bank reform. Kuhn, Loeb & Co. was sufficiently public-spirited about the matter to keep him on salary at 500,000 dollars per year while during the next six years he supposedly "donated" his time to the public good.

Working with Warburg in promoting this banking reform was Nelson Aldrich, known as Morgan's floor broker in the U.S. Senate. Aldrich's daughter Abby married John D. Rockefeller, Jr.

Aldrich was appointed by the Senate to head the National Monetary Commission, though he had little banking knowledge. Family ties and economic-banking ties finally brought together the famous and yet secretive meeting of bankers and politicians to Jekyll Island in 1910 to form a decision based on accumulated knowledge and experience of banking leaders—namely, that this nation needed a central bank.

They decided, because of past and present opposition by knowledgeable members of the Senate and other opposing bankers, not to call it a central bank. It had to be called some sort of "Regional Reserve Bank."

Out of the Jekyll Island meeting of international bankers came the proposal backed by some senators (for their own good) to form the Federal Reserve System.

This was all supposedly done to stop bank runs, to stop problems of locally run banks, and to consolidate banking for the good of the nation and the government.

Through much subtlety and trickery, the bill was finally put through by a vote of 268 to 60 on December 22, 1913, while most members of Congress were anxious to adjourn for Christmas and get home.

In addition to the above-mentioned individuals, Colonel Edward Mandel House was one of the main engineers of the Federal Reserve System, having worked closely with Woodrow Wilson for years in order to get it established.

House, according to his own writings, was one of the authors of America's graduated income tax, of the Federal Reserve System as a privately owned central bank, and of a flexible, inflatable currency for America. Colonel House and Warburg worked hand in hand to establish the Federal Reserve System in the United States.

Henry Cabot Lodge, Sr., proclaimed with great foresight and insight, "This bill as it stands seems to me to open the way to vast expansion [inflation] of the currency. I do not like to think that any law can be passed which will make it possible to submerge the gold standard in a flood of irredeemable paper currency" (*Congressional Record*, June 10, 1932).

The Federal Reserve System's first board was hand-picked by Colonel House, and he immediately placed Paul Warburg on the original board! It was set up as (and still is) a privately owned, and privately run system of money supply for the government and member banks.

How powerful is this organization today? Let's quote from the congressional report of Congressman Wright Patman (in his writings to the Subcommittee on Domestic Finance, Committee on Banking and Currency—House of Representatives, 88th Congress).

"In the United States today we have in effect two governments . . . We have the duly constituted government . . . and then we have an independent, uncontrolled, and uncoordinated government in the Federal Reserve System, operating the money powers which are reserved to Congress by the Constitution of the United States."

In October 1980, President Jimmy Carter publicly stated his opposition to the setting of interest rates and the making of decisions at this time by the Federal Reserve System, contrary to what he believed was best for the country.

FACT 7—OTHER ORGANIZED EFFORTS HAVE PRECEDED AND FOLLOWED THE FEDERAL RESERVE SYSTEM. THE ESTABLISHMENT OF THE SYSTEM WAS THE CULMINATION OF TWO CENTURIES OF EFFORT BY GLOBAL MANAGERS WHO WANT ONE-WORLD GOVERNMENT THROUGH MONETARY POWERS.

Meyer Amschel Rothschild once said about governments and monetary power, "Give me the power to coin money and set its value, and I care not who makes the laws."

Control of the nations of the world through a world government, one-world money, and a one-world government board of governors has been the goal of several groups down through the last 200 years. It all started with a man who organized the group called the Illuminati in 1776—The Order of the Illuminati. They were crushed in 1786 and went underground. Later they were called The League of Just Men. All groups involved still believe in the power of money to bring about a one-world government.

Still later, in the days of the Rothschilds, about 100 years after the crushing of the Order of the Illuminati, came the Round Table Group in England, which also branched into the Royal Institute of International Affairs. This was established in Canada as well.

In the United States they set up the Council on

Foreign Relations at 68th Street and Park Avenue, across from the Russian Embassy to the United Nations.

According to Professor Quigley, the Royal Institute for International Affairs and the Council on Foreign Relations were originally planned and drawn up in secret meetings in Paris.

This all happened in 1919, and was led primarily by the European banking groups, who wished to establish themselves more clearly in the United States in order to work on government policies here as well. The CFR (Council on Foreign Relations) was the offshot of the RIIA (Royal Institute for International Affairs).

Many of these *same original families* which promoted the Council on Foreign Relations in the U.S.A. were involved in promoting the Federal Reserve System in 1913, and some of the same names appear on government files as supporting the Bolshevik Revolution in Russia.

FACT 8—THE COUNCIL ON FOREIGN RELATIONS STUDIES FOREIGN AFFAIRS EXCLUSIVELY, AND BECAUSE OF THEIR EXPERTISE THEY OCCUPY IMPORTANT POSITIONS IN THE PRESIDENT'S CABINET.

A new book on all the president's men should be written about the regime of President Jimmy Carter. Heading the list would be Zbigniew Brzezinski, National Security Advisor. Born a Polish Jew, Brzezinski escaped the Holocaust and immigrated to the United States. Brzezinski's power and influence in Foreign Affairs has been extremely important. Cyrus Vance resigned as secretary of state because of strong differences with him. Brzezinski was educated in foreign affairs largely through the Council on

Foreign Relations. He was the first chairman of the new organization entitled the Trilateral Commission. This is the man who had the ear of the President of the United States, and he stated in his own writings in 1970 *(Between Two Ages)* that he believed in one-world government and in the final dissolving of nation-states and their sovereignties!

Paul Volcker came to the chairmanship of the Federal Reserve Board as a member of the Council on Foreign Relations and the Trilateral Commission. He came as the one man who pushed off the demonetization of gold when he was president of the New York City Reserve Bank—the most powerful of the 12 regional banks outside the Fed itself.

Volcker has been against gold backing of the dollar. All international banking establishments are against gold backing of the dollar (or of any other currency, for that matter), for gold backing *determines how much money can be created in cash and credit.* The Fed was once partly limited in money creation by the U.S. holdings of gold at Fort Knox, but this is no longer the case. That is why there was terrific inflation in the 70's. (Gold was demonitized in 1971.)

Many members of President Reagan's Cabinet, secretaries, under secretaries, and staff members came from the CFR or the Trilateral Commission.

FACT 9—THE OPINION OF THE COUNCIL ON FOREIGN RELATIONS IS THAT THE WORLD WILL BE BETTER WHEN IT HAS A SOCIALIST ONE-WORLD GOVERNMENT.

Study No. 7 published by the Council on Foreign Relations on November 25, 1959, states, " . . . building a new international order which must be responsive to world aspirations for peace and for social and economic change ... an international order ... including states labeling themselves as 'Socialist.'"

The ideals of the original groups in Europe are now part and parcel of the CFR and are being implemented extremely successfully in the White House to date.

Foreign policymaking is determined and controlled largely by members of the CFR, and thus the ideas inculcated in them are becoming the plan of our nation.

FACT 10—THE CFR IN COLLABORATION WITH THE BILDERBURGERS OF EUROPE DEVELOPED THE NEWLY FORMED TRILATERAL COMMISSION IN 1973.

Zbigniew Brzezinski was its first chairman after the origin by David Rockefeller. Carter and Mondale were charter members, having been invited to a charter meeting in London in 1973.

Antony Sutton, author of the book *Trilaterals over Washington*, states about this group: "The basic Trilateral Commission structure is a power pyramid. At the tip of the pyramid we can identify a 'financial mafia,' comprising several old-line American families—the American Aristocracy. Below this highest level is the Executive Committee for the U.S., linked to members of the Executive Committees in Europe and Japan. Next comes the Trilateral Commission itself: 109 members from Canada and the United States, 106 from Europe, and 74 from Japan."

Trilaterals virtually controlled the executive branch of U.S. government under Carter, and so controlled much policy. An ongoing program or project is to dominate nine crucial countries in Europe and Japan, and by virtue of their productive capacity account for 80 percent of the total world output. This "core" group can then dominate the remaining 20 percent of the world fairly easily. The American multinationals provide country-by-country liaison, intelligence, and conduits, the sinews which bind a global new world order to the directions of the financial mafia.

Sutton says that the Trilaterals have rejected the U.S. Constitution (and the Canadian form of government) as well as the democratic political process, and that their objective is to obtain the wealth of the world for their own use under the pretext of public service.

On pages 36 and 37 of my book *How to Survive the Money Crash* you can read further on the Trilateral Commission and its Canadian, American European, and Japanese membership, with the names of the parties involved.

President Reagan's Cabinet has Casper Weinberger and General Haig as two of his aides, along with many others in the Cabinet who are members of the Council on Foreign Relations and the Trilateral Commission.

3

The Real Power of Money

FACT 11—WHOEVER CONTROLS THE IS-
SUANCE OF MONEY CAN VIRTUALLY CON-
TROL WHAT A GOVERNMENT DOES.

As Meyer Amschel Rothschild once said, "Give me
the power to coin money and I care not who makes
the laws."

Money is power, but it is not true wealth in itself,
strictly speaking. Money buys power, and of course it
buys wealth. Wealth is stored up and/or is real estate
ownership, gold and silver ownership, jewels, art,
commodities, food, and products that have value
because they are in demand by the consumers of the
world (as in land itself). This is real wealth.

Money, whatever form it takes, is a means to ac-
quiring real wealth and, along with it, real power.

If a government cannot get money it cannot carry
out its plans for the nation. Plans for new programs
have to be scrapped. Perhaps existing programs cannot be financed either, and have to be cut back.

This has always been part of the argument for the
demonetization of gold. As long as gold was required
to back the dollar in the U.S., the dollar was as strong
as gold and could not be printed or created in credit
forms for the government beyond the value of the
gold deposits on hand in Fort Knox.

The original Constitution of the United States called

for the coining of money, not the printing of paper money (though it had been tried before). Our founding fathers committed to Congress the power to create money and to determine its value.

The power to coin money was never intended to be given to the central bankers or to the privately owned Fed, but only to Congress, as Congressman Putman has pointed out in his statements and literature on money.

International bankers wanted control of the American money supply (as they had in Europe), but they did not get it at the time. They got it in 1913 in the establishment of the Federal Reserve System, with their own men controlling it.

Their powers were greatly enhanced and broadened after the manipulated 1929-33 crash. Since then their rapidly expanding power base around the world has become so powerful through the organizations that we have described as to be unbelievable to most people who hear of them.

International bankers pushed for the removal of gold from behind the dollar in the U.S. and in the currencies of other nations. They succeeded in stripping gold and silver of their monetary value as far as banking circles are concerned.

No longer is gold necessary to back our money. Thus, the money supply can be increased as governments wish, as politicians desire, or as the central banks of various nations can arrange with the governments to increase it.

This is true not only in the United States and many nations of Europe, but also in new nations that appear on the horizon in Africa, and elsewhere. The international bankers are there, telling the new leaders about the "established policy" of world bankers and nations everywhere—namely, that of letting the bankers create the money supply and hopefully determining the interest rates for each nation as well.

FACT 12—MONEY IS PRINTED BY A PRIVATE COMPANY FOR MANY NATIONS IN EUROPE, AND THE MONEY SUPPLY AND INTEREST RATES ARE CONTROLLED OR INFLUENCED BY CENTRAL BANKERS IN MOST FREE-WORLD NATIONS.

It is by the De La Rue Company in England that over 60 nations have their money printed for them and shipped directly to them, including most of the nations of the world that are most familiar to all of us.

In the U.S. the money is printed in the U.S. Treasury, which is owned by the government, but the *amount* of money created is determined by the Federal Reserve System and Board.

Gary Allen reminds us: "The House hearings on stabilization of the purchasing power of the dollar disclosed evidence in 1928 that the Federal Reserve Board was working closely with the heads of European Central Banks. The Committee warned that a major crash had been planned in 1927. Shortly after this *warning*, the Federal Reserve Board reversed its easy-money position, which had previously been used for the development of the country and the advancement of the stock market."

Suddenly, it began raising the discount rate, late in 1929.

William Bryan describes what happened in his writings of The United States Unresolved Monetary and Political Problems.

"When everything was ready, the New York financiers started calling the 24-hour broker call loans. This meant that the stock brokers and the customers had to dump their stock on the market in order to pay the loans (that were being called in at that time by the Fed). This naturally collapsed the stock market and brought about the banking collapse all over the two countries, because the banks not owned by the oligarchy were heavily involved in broker call claims at this time, and bank runs soon exhausted their coin and currency supplies and they had to close. The Federal Reserve System would not come to their aid, although they were instructed under law to maintain an elastic currency."

The Federal Reserve System caused the 1929 collapse. They can do it again when it suits their purpose.

It should be noted that the big boys were out of the stock market by September 1929, before it collapsed on October 29, 1929. They sold out, got their high prices before the market fell, and bought back in again later, making phenomenal profits.

Congressman Louis McFadden, Chairman of the House Banking and Currency Committee, said in the Congressional Record:

"It was not accidental. It was a carefully contrived occurence. The international bankers sought to bring about a condition of despair here (and in Canada) so that they might emerge as the rulers of all."

FACT 13—EACH RECESSION IN THE U.S. AND CANADA SINCE 1929 HAS FOLLOWED TWO THINGS: 1) AN INCREASE IN THE MONEY SUPPLY AND LOWER INTEREST RATES; AND 2) A DECREASE IN THE MONEY SUPPLY AND STAGGERING INCREASES IN INTEREST RATES.

It is happening again right now in unprecedented form and fashion.

Check the following facts: Every time the stock market falls greatly, there is an increase in the interest rates for general business, making money very tight. In addition, this amounts to deflation of normally available money. Every time there is a good increase in the stock market earnings, it follows a period when the money flowed freely through lessened interest rates, and there was plenty of money for business expansion.

The recession of 1973 had this same cause, as did the depressed years of 1936-37, 1948, 1953, 1956-57, 1960, 1966, 1970, and now 1979-82.

This last recession signals us that big things are about to happen, now that things have gone this far. International bankers are getting ready for the one-world global government.

FACT 14—THERE IS A DEPRESSION COMING THROUGH INTEREST RATES AND INFLATION THAT WILL BE BLAMED ON AN OIL EMBARGO BY THE ARABS.

Someone will have to take the blame so that the elite will be respected and extolled as our economic saviors.

Why not blame the Arabs? They have the black gold—oil—and can easily be maneuvered into complete compliance with the Trilaterals for a large piece of the global pie thereafter.

In collaboration with the Arab members of OPEC (over the Israeli situation) it would not be hard to organize another depression in North America.—*even without Europe being too involved*—by means of an oil shutoff.

Without oil, our industry and nation will grind to a halt. Canada will be somewhat better off, with the Alberta oil fields pumping steadily. The U.S. could make it without Arab oil, but international interests have caused legislation to be passed in Washington that delays and even cancels the development of nuclear power in this country, the offshore drilling of wells, and the release of oil from shale.

FACT 15—HIGH INTEREST RATES CAN KILL A COUNTRY IN A SHORT TIME. HIGH INTEREST RATES ARE FAR WORSE THAN INFLATION.

In the United States (as in other nations) the Central Bank, which is the Federal Reserve System, affects interest rates every three weeks or so in Washington D.C., through a board known as the Open Market Committee.

Perhaps we should let Congressman Wright Patman tell us about this from his Primer on Money presented to the Committee on Banking and Currency for the United States Government.

"The Open Market Committee, as it is called, decides only what the maximum amount of money shall be; it cannot determine that the actual maximum amount of money will be created. It is a committee made up of 12 members. There are the 7 members of the board of governors plus 5 of 12 presidents of the Federal Reserve Banks. Congress assumed when it established the committee in the 1933-35 era that the public members, with a 7-5 majority, would control the Committee. As for voting, the President of the New York Federal Reserve Bank always has a vote, the Cleveland and Chicago presidents vote in alternate years, and the presidents of other Federal Reserve Banks are voting members every third year. Since the New York president and seven governors always are voting members of the Committee, there are eight permanent voting memberships and four rotating memberships."

The point that Congressman Patman is making is that the whole board was and is riddled with private-interest powers, who make policy for the whole nation financially under the guise of serving the people of the government, while in reality they have the power to serve themselves and their own banking interests.

FACT 16—CENTRAL BANKS (IN OUR CASE THE FEDERAL RESERVE SYSTEM) ENCOURAGE LAVISH GOVERNMENT SPENDING.

As the banker of first resort to the government of the lands they represent, central banks and their bankers love big governmental budgets, and they encourage governments to spend as much as possible, since it is these bankers who lend the money to the government. Then the government, through subsequent taxation of the people for years to come, has to pay the money back to the Federal Reserve System.

Big government budgets mean much borrowing by the government from the central bankers. In the U.S. the government runs the Treasury, where the money is printed, even though it is ordered by the Fed for the government as the government confers with the liaison board for the system.

The U.S. government determines weekly what it will need from the Federal Reserve System. It then contacts the proper channels—the Secretary of the Treasury and the Federal Reserve Board.

The Board then relays to the system what the government needs. The Board acts as liaison between the system and the government. The Board then orders the Treasury to print or create the credit money which the government needs.

The government then sells to the system, via the New York brokers, the bonds that the government has created for the exchange of money from the system for government use.

The Federal Reserve Board then sells the bonds, collects the interest in over 21 bond markets in New York City, and keeps the money for the operation of the system.

The government gets the money, the system gets the bonds (plus interest), and everyone is happy—especially the owners and investors of the system.

Now the government has to pay off those bonds one way or another, at one time or another, to either the primary owner or the secondary, or so on. Taxpayers' money pays off the bonds to the owners, with the interest specified on the bond itself.

It is in the financial interest of the Fed and the bankers to have big government budgets, and also to demonetize gold in every country possible.

When money creation is no longer limited by the amount of gold in the treasury, politicians plan bigger budgets, spend more money on their constituencies, throw more money overseas, and in general adopt measures to spend billions of dollars never available before.

It took the U.S. 200 years to get a government budget of 300 billion dollars. It took the Carter Administration and Congress 3½ years to double it to 662 billion dollars and more!

How did this happen?

The demonetization of gold was the number one reason.

Lobbyists, who are highly skilled negotiators, planners and promoters, lobby daily for programs that cost billions in Washington.

Promises are made to the politicians pushing legislation for these lobbyists, and thus up go the budgets, up goes billion-dollar spending, up goes the revenue to the Federal Reserve System, and up goes the incredible weekly debt of the U.S. government to the Fed and others.

FACT 17—THE FEDERAL OPEN-MARKET COMMITTEE SETS THE MAXIMUM AMOUNT OF GOVERNMENT SECURITIES TO BE PURCHASED OR SOLD, THUS DETERMINING THE AMOUNT OF THE OVERALL MONEY SUPPLY. THIS AFFECTS WHAT THE INTERNATIONAL BANKERS OF NEW YORK CITY DO WITH RESPECT TO THE PRIME INTEREST RATE FOR THE NATION'S BUSINESS ACTIVITY.

Though the Open Market Committee does not determine the final prime interest rate (which is set by the megabankers), it does affect it by determining how many government securities will be purchased, thus raising *reserves* or high-powered money in the money-creation system.

The Fed buys government securities and thus increases reserves throughout the system. This means there can be a general increase in the money supply as checks are drawn and deposited in banks, and the system of money creation takes place.

As reserves are placed in the banks, they can create 12 times the amount of money they have in the new reserves, or whatever the determination for reserve requirements calls for.

We will cover this further in the next point, but remember that business activity is created by available money for the nation.

Money is created by buying government securities, either by the Fed or by privately owned commercial banks.

If the Fed buys them, the interest earned after Fed operational expenses goes back to the government Treasury. If the commercial banks of the nation buy them, the interest is paid directly to them.

This makes a terrific difference in the government debt.

If the Open Market Committee determines that the money supply will be increased heavily, then international bankers can actually set the prime rate up, knowing that they will be affecting what the government has to pay them when they buy government securities next week. It is a money game, played out to the fullest, making the U.S. government the victim at the taxpayers' expense.

It is the greatest transfer of wealth known in history. Money is being transferred through taxation and inflation (the hidden tax) to the non-productive sector from the productive sector. Money-earners lose to the money-getters.

FACT 18—THE MONEY SUPPLY IS DIRECTLY DETERMINED BY BUYING GOVERNMENT SECURITIES AND BY SETTING RESERVE REQUIREMENTS FOR THE BANKS. THIS DETERMINES HOW MUCH MONEY PRIVATE BANKS CAN CREATE AND THE FED CREATES. THUS BUSINESS ACTIVITY IS DIRECTLY RELATED TO WHAT 12 MEN DECIDE IN WASHINGTON (PLUS THE INTERNATIONAL BANKERS) WITH RESPECT TO INTEREST RATES.

The megabankers create the interest rates for available money, but the Federal Reserve Board determines the actual amount of cash and credit money that is created weekly by determining the reserve requirements for banks.

Banks are in the business of creating and loaning money. They create now on a basis of 12 new dollars for every dollar they hold in reserve, or whatever the Fed states that they do. Reserve requirements may change daily, and often do change that often. As banks adhere to the set reserve requirements for the week, so money is created by the high-powered dollars that they keep in reserve.

The Fed can change the money supply by either lowering or raising reserve requirements in local banks or by buying and/or selling government securities.

Raising reserve requirements means less money available for loaning out—illiquidity. Lowering reserves means the opposite—liquidity.

By buying government securities the Fed creates the check with which they are purchased out of nothing. That is money creation. Then the check is eventually deposited in a commercial bank somewhere, which makes it high-powered money out of which more money is created.

As the government demands money for monetization of debts (by selling securities in the open market) the government forces up the money supply astronomically and is the chief executioner of the economic system of the United States.

President Reagan's budget will reach one trillion dollars annually by 1984-85.

4

The Shocking Truth About Banking Procedures

FACT 19—MONEY IS A MANUFACTURED ITEM. IT CAN BE IN CASH OR CREDIT. THE AMOUNT OF MONEY TO BE MADE AVAILABLE TO THE NATION AND THE GOVERNMENT IS DETERMINED BY ITS MANUFACTURES.

Under the Constitution of the United States of America, only Congress has the power to coin money. But Congress long ago farmed out this responsibility to the Federal Reserve System, the Central Bank of America, which is the bank supplying the government with money.

The Fed has to supply all the needs of government as ordered. The government raises money through taxation and by the selling of securities, bonds, etc. to anyone who will buy them, including the Fed.

More of this will be discussed later, but at this point it is only important to realize that the government budget is set by Congress and the President and not by the Fed. What securities the government does not sell to businesses, individuals, etc. the Fed has to buy, and thus it is the Fed's responsibility to create the cash or credit money for the government to monetize its debts and pay for its current programs.

But in addition the Fed also has the power to lower or raise the money supply for the nation by determining the reserve requirements for banks monthly.

If the Fed believes it is in the interest of all to let the money supply flow freely, it can lower the reserve requirements that commercial banks of the nation must hold (on the fractional reserve system). (Each bank has to hold a fraction in cash or securities of what they are going to create and loan out on paper—more on this later.)

If the Fed believes (as lately) that the nation is better served by less money supplied, then the reserve requirements go up higher and higher, and less money is created by the commerical banks and thus less is loaned out.

The Open Market Committee move on reserve requirements affects what the giant banks set as their prime rate for that period. Lately money is tight (illiquidity), and thus the prime rate is up. If you borrow money, you must pay dearly for it.

The Fed has been granted the independent power to increase or decrease the money supply for the nation. If this concurs with what Congress and the President want, good. If not, the Fed has the power to do what it wishes anyway.

This affects you and me tremendously, as we shall see more clearly shortly.

The history behind this power is simply that originally banking in the nation and money creation was the sole responsibility of individual banks in whatever state they were. Banks created their own notes—money. That was fine as long as it was a small enough community and everyone accepted the local bank money. But when industry developed and business expanded from state to state, one bank would be reluctant to accept another bank's money. This started to breed real trouble for the nation's businesses, and even for the farmers.

We were primarily an agricultural community at

first. As business and industry grew, so did demand for a uniform currency for the entire country.

International bankers capitalized on this desire, and along with creating banking panics in the late 1880's and early 1900's, they pushed for legislation, through their powerful insiders and lobbyists, for a uniform money and a central bank to issue it.

The word was out that the only way this nation would survive economically was to have a central bank and a unified currency, and "Let the experts do it."

This came about in 1913 (as described earlier), although certain senators plus President Woodrow Wilson felt that to let one bank do it all would be to put our nation into the hands of men who might fall prey to the temptation to be self-serving. So 12 regional Federal Reserve Banks were set up, each with the power to create money (cash and credit) for each region of the United States, thus decentralizing the power of money creation by placing each bank in virtual competition with the other (rather than in competetive unity, as they are now).

This was a start for the central bankers, but it was not all that they wanted. They wanted one bank to have the supreme powers of money creation for the government and the nations's needs.

FACT 20—THE GREAT DEPRESSION OF THE EARLY 30's WAS PLANNED AND COOR-DINATED BY THE INTERNATIONAL BANKERS TO PUSH FOR FURTHER POWERS IN THE BANKING WORLD OF AMERICA. THEY GOT WHAT THEY WANTED.

Finally, in the aftermath of the terrible depression, which was planned and coordinated on time by the insiders (with much suffering to both local bankers and citizenry), in 1933 Roosevelt pushed for new powers to unify the money-creation system in Washington D.C., consisting of one central bank with 12 regional offices to coordinate and funnel money to the commercial banks of the states and the national banks of the country.

Between 1933 and 1935 legislation was passed enabling the central bank to take complete authority for money creation. The bankers had been pushing for this for over 100 years, and with determined persistence they attained their monetary goal here even as they had in other countries (as in Canada and Europe).

FACT21—INDIVIDUAL BANKS WERE CHARTERED BY THE GOVERNMENT AND STILL ARE TO SERVE THEIR LOCAL COMMUNITIES AND TO BUILD AND STRENGTHEN LOCAL BUSINESS, BUT BANKS HAVE BECOME LESS AND LESS INTERESTED IN THIS. THEY ARE NOW USING THEIR MONEY-CREATING POWER TO PURCHASE SHORT AND LONG-TERM U.S. GOVERNMENT AND TAX-FREE MUNICIPAL BONDS.

The purchasing of government securities and municipal bonds by the local banker is more profitable and requires less paperwork and effort by the local banker. He is interested in making money for his bank. He is looking at his bank earnings more than at serving the community. Banks have to make a profit, but the tendency lately has been to overlook the needs of some community members and instead to buy what is profitable for the bank.

What are now multinational banks of the United States started as smaller community-servicing banks. They grew to immense proportions through business expertise and also through a greedy desire to promote one-world govenment via banking control and money manipulation.

Multinational banks of America today are often guilty, through their offshore branches, of selling out the dollar at times when the nation needs them and their expertise to strengthen the dollar by holding it. Instead, when they think dollars will dip in value on the international market they sell high, causing a deep dip. In the final analysis they hurt everyone except themselves.

It appears now that the multinational banks not only want to capitalize on the growth and wealth of this country, but they do not care what happens in the final analysis, for one-world banking control over all industrialized nations appeals to their baser motives.

FACT 22—TWO CONTROL CENTERS IN THE UNITED STATES (AS IN OTHER COUNTRIES) DETERMINE ECONOMIC POLICY. ONE IS THE GOVERNMENT WITH ITS BUDGET AND THE OTHER IS THE INDEPENDENT FEDERAL RESERVE SYSTEM. OFTEN THEY OPPOSE EACH OTHER IN PLANNING AND PROGRAMMING FOR THE NATION'S ECONOMY.

With the enlarged powers of the Fed in 1933 and 1935 giving them control through a single central bank (dwarfing the original idea of President Wilson to have 12 separate banks serving their areas) and with the public power gone out of the privately controlled Open Market Committee, we have established a monetary power base in this nation that can act in opposition to the government if it wishes to.

Often it does. When President Carter was running for reelection he declared that the monetary policies of the Fed were running contrary to what he wanted and needed for reelection.

Interest rates were set astronomically high. Business was suppressed and unemployment was running much higher than when he was first elected. Business bankruptcies prevailed, the marketplace was hurting badly, and the recession was in full swing, with the auto, steel, and building industries hurting the worst since the Great Depression. All this hurt Carter badly in his bid for reelection.

The Federal Reserve System and the Fed Board elected to raise interest rates twice during the year of 1980, and they also greatly increased the money supply.

The increase in the money supply was done by the sale of government securities, thereby increasing the billions in the Fed reserves. The high interest rates did not in any way cut into the inflation rates, but they fatally affected business development in the nation.

This Fed activity was all done in the supposed interest of reducing the inflation rate, but it did not and will not do so. You cannot produce high interest rates only to decrease the inflation of the nation. You must suppress the money supply by applying monetary brakes to the presses through the Federal Government's budget plans.

One without the other is futile. We have proven that. It requires monetary as well as fiscal control to stop inflation—not just high interest rates, which only stop business development.

The original free and private enterprise system of the United States was set up to develop business and farming as big as the law of supply and demand would enable it to grow. The bigger the better. The bigger business was, the more people could be employed. The more immigrants would be welcome with their skills to this great nation. It worked perfectly, in contrast to other monetary-government situations in dictatorships, socialistic societies, and Communist countries. Our system really worked. Millions were put to work. Government regulations were at a minimum, and money flowed as need demanded.

FACT 23—WHEN MULTINATIONAL BANKERS (WHO CONTROL THE FEDERAL RESERVE SYSTEM) PLAY WITH INTEREST RATES AND THE MONEY SUPPLY, THEY REGULATE THE UPS AND DOWNS OF THE STOCK MARKET AND THUS MAKE BILLIONS FOR THEM-SELVES.

There are at least two reasons for the misregulation of the nations's interest rates, and probably more.

First, when interest rates are up and then down and then up again, the stock market fluctuates terrifically. It drops and rises as the bankers manipulate the interest rates plus the money supply.

High interest rates cause big investors to buy government-guaranteed securities, producing a drop in stock-market investment. This means a drop in the Dow Jones Industrial Average.

Knowing when interest rates are going to rise, the insiders can sell stocks heavily while stocks are up. When the interest rates go up, the stocks fall. The insiders get out on time. They buy in again when the stock is low, and they stay in while it climbs (as interest rates go down again).

FACT 24—WHEN INTEREST RATES ARE UP, BUSINESS ACTIVITY AND GROWTH ARE DOWN. AS A CONSTANT DIET FOR AMERICA THIS WOULD LEAD THE NATION INTO

BUSINESS BANKRUPTCY AND THUS INTO AN ACCEPTANCE OF THE ONE-WORLD GOVERNMENT-BUSINESS SYSTEM.

Original efforts toward global management have failed and been delayed for many reasons. It appears not that the world is ready for monetary unification and government unity, and this is the opinion of the international groups promoting such unity.

Political weaknesses all over the world dictate to multinational orders that their time has come for world leadership.

FACT 25—IT IS AN INDISPUTABLE FACT THAT PRIVATE BANKING INTERESTS WIELD UNBELIEVABLE POWER WITHIN THE FEDERAL RESERVE BOARD AND OPEN MARKET COMMITTEE. THEY OFTEN MAKE SELF-SERVING DECISIONS RELATED TO THE AMOUNT OF MONEY SUPPLY.

The Open Market Committee that meets approximately every three weeks in Washington to determine the money supply and other monetary decisions is loaded with private interests, and thus loaded decisions are often made which benefit only the bankers, and not the public or private sectors of business in this nation.

It would be most unnatural for all of their decisions to be made purely in the nation's best interests. Human nature does not work that way!

Each of the 12 regional Federal Reserve Banks of the nation is operated by nine directors. Six of these nine for each of the banks are elected by the member banks of each region (tied into the Federal Reserve System in that geographical area).

The Open Market Committee is made up of the seven members of the Federal Reserve Board appointed by the President for 14 years. But the 12 presidents of the Regional Federal Reserve Banks also sit with the seven in total discussions of the money supply and the reserves that the Fed will buy from the government, which is always selling securities to someone to gain money for monetizing government debt. But when the Fed buys from the government, it is increasing reserves for member banks to create more money for banking purposes.

Nineteen men sit and discuss monetary policy every three weeks. But only five of the 12 regional presidents can finally vote for policy with the Federal Reserve Board, thus acting as a 12-man voting power.

It was actually to be a seven-man public majority over the five-man banking interests that was to control policy. The seven members were not to be members of the banking authority but were to be appointed by the President and ratified by the Congress to represent the nation's interests. They were careful back in Woodrow Wilson's day to set it up this way.

But now we have a president of the New York City Federal Reserve Bank, Mr. Paul Volcker, as the head of the Federal Reserve Board in Washington, sitting with six other men with presidential backing. Where did they come from? If the President would appoint a Fed bank president from New York City as president of the Fed in Washington, what would keep him from appointing along with him six other men who think alike? To what extent was the President encouraged to select men backed by the Council on Foreign Relations and the Trilateral Commission?

This needs investigating. It may very well turn out to be the greatest problem in the United States today.

But beyond the validity of that point is the fact that the Federal Open Market Committee does affect interest rates for the nation by determining the supply of money available to the nation's banks and consumers.

As they meet and study consumer demand for money plus the current rate of inflation, they determine the amount of government securities which the Fed will buy in order to build reserves for commercial banks to use.

The actions of this committee restricting credit or expanding it determine largely the rates that will be set by the big New York City banks for the prime rate.

Congressman Wright Patman said this:

"The Open Market Committee's authority over the nation's economic life and its influence over the nations position in world affairs lies in its power to determine this nation's credit policies. Determining credit policies means determining the nation's supply of money and credit, and therefore the general level of interest rates, among other things.

"There is no doubt about the influence of the Committee on interest rates. The Committee can and has changed the money supply at will to reach an interest rate objective.

"The price leaders, then, as far as interest rates are concerned, are the big New York banks, whose prime rate forms a base on which the nation's structure of interest rates rests. Changes in this prime rate signal bankers throughout the nation to raise or lower their rates accordingly.

"But what determines the prime rate? And what forces set off changes in that rate? The answer is that the few large New York banks set prime rate and change it—combining their feel of the supply and demand for credit with their knowledge and expectations about Treasury policy and Federal Reserve Open Market Committee policy."

At almost all times the Treasury of the United States government is borrowing huge amounts of money, usually to repay money which the government had borrowed previously. Government bonds and securities are always coming due, and of course have to be honored. The Secretary of the Treasury issues new certificates to replace the old. They are sold in New York, as are other securities for corporations. But as the Fed buys them, the price (interest rates paid by the government to the buyers of securities) is negotiated just prior to a Tuesday sale.

The interest rate charged is usually just below the prime rate set by the big New York banks for their prime rate. The higher the prime, the higher the rate the government has to pay.

Thus as the Open Market Committee makes its final decisions about the money supply and federal reserves required that month, the New York megabankers set their prime rate, affecting the cost of selling Treasury securities.

The stock markets of the world rise and fall only about 10 percent, based on business activity of the businesses and corporations involved in them. Over 90 percent of the reasons why the markets move so precariously at times is related to the money supply and interest rates, and thus the value of international currencies. (The latter is affected by the former two.)

Nothing is more important to any of us in the world of business than interest rates.

Those levels go back to the actions and decisions of the 12 men every month!

As interest rates fluctuate, so does investment profit. If one could know what the interest rates were going to do even short-term, he would invest accordingly and come out on top.

Does it seem strange to you that these clever money

manipulators seem to know what decisions are going to be made in the Open Market Committee and thus when to buy currencies on the foreign exchange themselves?

When interest rates are down and the dollar is weakened, they have already sold out of dollars and are into gold, etc.

When interest rates are up and the prime rate is high, and gold is weakened by those bailing out of it for another investment, we notice that the multinational banks, knowing what is happening, buy heavily into U.S. dollars *just before the rates go up*, allowing them to profit greatly on foreign-exchange markets.

Do you wonder why multinational banks suddenly sell off dollars in amounts of millions and instead buy foreign currency or gold and silver futures, when just a day or so later the dollar nosedives due to oversupply by the Fed?

If you controlled the interest rates of nations as a family of multinational bankers, you could know in plenty of time what was going to happen to the West German Mark, the English pound, the American dollar, etc. It is all planned by the money power brokers. They hold allegiance to no flag and constitution and pay no homage to any political leaders. They are their own nationality and breed. They worship money and political power.

FACT 26—NOT ONLY DO INTERNATIONAL BANKERS WORK TO AFFECT AND CONTROL THE U.S.A.'s COMMITTEE DETERMINING THE PRICE OF THEIR MONEY, BUT THEY ARE ALSO CONNECTED WITH PRIVATE BANKING OFFICIALS, WHO SET THE PRICE FOR THEIR PRODUCT ABROAD.

There is an international family of megabankers attempting to control central banks and committees similar to our own Open Market Committee in nation after nation around the world.

In many cases they are the committees and boards governing the interest rates and the nation's money supply as the so called experts of monetary control. They encourage government selling of bonds and securities in every nation they enter. The deeper the government debt to them the greater control they will eventually (if not currently) wield.

If the Western nations are to have a completely new order of government at the right time, then simultaneous actions have to be produced in them, actions which are timed just right.

Money manipulation and the setting of interest rates in one country can come at a time which coincides with the interest rates of another nation so as to bring about the greatest profit to the foreign-exchange buyers of the families involved.

Unquestionably there is now a power war going on between the money brokers of the world.

Europe has its own plan for world control, as do the U.S. counterparts, with their interests in Canada also.

Who will win?

Possibly, because of the power of the dollar, Europe will not be able to gain control internationally without including the U.S. power magnates.

The Europeans have set up ECU—European Currency Unit—as a monetary unified system of the Common Market in order to ultimately take the place of the dollar as the world's reserve currency, should it be necessary at the downfall of the dollar.

To what extent the Rockefeller clan are in on this ECU movement is not too well known. They could eventually cooperate or they could try it on their own, fueling the battle between the world powers of the Rothschilds and the Rockefellers.

Chase Manhattan attempted "forex" money in 1980 as a Foreign Exchange Money account held at Chase for larger investors. This seemed in opposition to what the Europeans were trying to do. Only time will tell about their unification or further competitive division.

FACT 27—BANKS HAVE THE POWER TO CREATE THEIR OWN CASH AND CREDIT, MADE POSSIBLE BY CONGRESSIONAL LEGISLATION. THEY OPERATE ON THE FRACTIONAL RESERVE SYSTEM, USING HIGH-POWERED DOLLARS TO CREATE MANY MORE DOLLARS OUT OF NOTHING.

Before Abraham Lincoln's administration, the private commercial banks of the nation were permitted to issue paper money, today called state bank notes. This meant that any group of businessmen obtaining a state charter for a local bank (as they complied with regulations for the forming of the same) could issue notes and print currency as money.

State bank notes disappeared shortly after the government passed the National Bank Act of 1863. This act canceled out the state system of money creation and gave to the federal government the powers that president Lincoln wanted them to have. They empowered federally chartered private banks to create currency and had them operate under federal regulations for the creation of national bank notes instead of the state notes (used rather indiscriminately previously).

Industrialization of the nation demanded a uniform currency and a National Bank Act. Later, when President Woodrow Wilson set up the Fed, in 1913, the government withdrew the national bank's privilege of creating banknote currency.

Now it was the responsibility of the Fed to completely unify the system of money creation.

The government under the direction of the international bankers allowed the Fed to set up a fractional reserve system, which simply means that the banks had to hold only a fraction of their deposits on hand in case depositors demanded their money. The bankers used these deposits as "high-powered money." For each dollar on deposit they could create six more dollars in "bookkeeping money" that they could use to loan out (on paper only) to would-be borrowers. The high-powered dollars actually existed. The bookkeeping money did not exist. But the consumer did not have to know that.

The bookkeeping money brought interest at a nominal rate in those days, and the borrower returned to the bank (the lender) actual dollars in repayment of the principal, plus the interest. Banks made money because they could create something out of nothing in the very beginning. This was what the original "gold holder" or "goldsmith" did back in the 1600's when he held gold and silver for the owners and used it as a basis for loans. He learned that only a few of the real owners came in at any particular time to take out all their money.

Today about 80 percent of all money is simply bookkeeping money, commonly called "computer digital inputs." It doesn't exist in actual physical form; it exists as computer digits.

Banks and consumers need only about 20 percent of the money supply to be in cash form for small business transactions. Today we use credit cards and checks for exchange of money for goods. It is easier and somewhat safer.

We normally use small amounts of cash for smaller needs, such as gas, groceries, and small-change items such as entertainment, etc.

State banks do not any longer create state notes or bank notes, but they create bank deposits from their depositors' money through the fractional reserve system.

Congress in collaboration with the Fed stated that a 6-to-1 fractional reserve was acceptable.

1980 legislation promoted by President Carter and pushed by the international bankers has brought some shocking and perhaps devastating new powers to the Federal Reserve System. The power we view under this point is that they now *only have to have one dollar for every 12 dollars they create on the fractional reserve system.*

This is inflationary, to say the least. Now for every dollar in reserve, 12 more hypothetical dollars are created for loans and interest. The rich are getting richer and the poor are getting poorer!

The bankers can create more money from nothing and make much more than ever before in history—*at a time when inflation is growing fast enough in this country to put hundreds of thousands of businesses into bankruptcy every year!*

There is no question that this legislation was promoted internally by the Trilateral Commission through its insiders in the President's Cabinet and through the Fed itself.

It is a devastating piece of action that we will get back to next. But for here let us continue with the specific point of the fractional reserve system and how much money is created, whether in cash or in credit by computers.

The advantage of the fractional reserve system is twofold. First it puts men into the banking business to make a profit, which is the reason for being in any business. Second, it provides money for businesses and the advancement of new enterprises in a locality (regulated by law), as the banker feels the borrower deserves.

The dangers of the fractional reserve system were originally that the holders of gold overreacted to the idea and could be hung for not having enough funds on hand to satisfy the cash needs of depositors. If a depositor came in and demanded a large amount of money out of the hands of the banker and he did not have it, or if many people came in and demanded their funds and he was too loaned out, he was bankrupt and out of business as a banker. Hanging was a result in many cases.

FACT 28—GOVERNMENT DEBT MEANS GREATER AND GREATER CREDIT BEING EXTENDED TO THE GOVERNMENT. AN INCREASE OF 80 BILLION DOLLARS A YEAR TO THE GOVERNMENT BUDGET MEANS GREATER AND GREATER INFLATION, FOR INFLATION AT THAT LEVEL BEGINS TO FEED ON ITSELF. GREATER GOVERNMENT DEBT MEANS GREATER INFLATION LEVELS FOR THE NATION, INFLATION THEN FEEDS INFLATION AS A CAUSE-AND-EFFECT CYCLE. THE ONLY END TO THIS IS A COLLAPSE OF THE GOVERNMENT DEBT.

Add to this fact the staggering private-sector debt and credit buying of today. We have then a credit collapse on our hands, since we can only stretch the credit dollar so far, and then it loses its elasticity, along with the printed dollar.

We have an inverted pyramid of debt, as in the case of any big spender and small earner.

At some point the pyramid of debt will tilt and drop over in a major correction. We can only support so much debt—then comes the correction, or payday. Payday will be an inevitable depression, which is a synonym for correction of prices.

Because the debt pyramid is supported by inflation, inflation feeds on itself and thus creates inequities everywhere. The transfer of wealth from earners to takers (by creating joblessness and lack of productivity and products) gives the nation a spurt of higher prices of a hitherto unheard-of level. Prices reach dizzying heights while inflation is feeding itself.

But the inflation tower must fall, and those who are victims of this terrible waste and displacement of talent are the consumers, who will wind up with a million babbling tongues about who and what caused it all.

Each recession, as it comes because of inflation, means that the government must restimulate the economy with a fresh dose of inflation—more money. With each dose come rising wages and prices and thus even more inflation. How many ingenious ways can the government invent until the bust? I believe they are now running out of stimulative answers.

Government-created jobs are not working. Wage and price controls never work. They always work in reverse of what is desired.

We are down to either cutting the budget or using interest rates and reduced liquidity to cut consumer inflation, with short bursts of liquidity to reduce the recession, until the end comes as man on deathbed takes transfusions, shots, etc., to keep him alive, until these things no longer keep his life-support systems alive and functioning. The economy of the United States and the Western nations is as above—the dying man is being shot, plugged, transfused, injected, and operated on, but it is all too cosmetic and too late. Death is coming.

The only question in the mind of most economists today is *when.*

I think it is possible that it could come overnight, if the Arabs precipitate it by pulling the oil rug out from underneath us.

That would do it, along with withdrawing their vast amounts of dollars from our banks.

If that does not happen, we could go for another three or four years with inflation and interest rates going up and down, and then will come the last down.

It will be severe. Are you ready for it?

Keep in mind that with greater and greater inflation the consumers of the nation have to earn more and more to keep up with the spiraling prices that come as a result of inflation. But how do they do that? Inflation is outpacing income rises three to one.

Thus consumer debt is increasing, consumer credit is increasing, and consumer income as related to inflation is lessening in terms of purchasing power. Consumer savings are at an all-time low while consumer purchasing power is slipping rapidly.

No doubt the answer will come when the savings are depleted and the limit is reached in consumer credit. Then will be the depression.

The consumer debt (credit buying) was 25 times larger in the last half of the 70's than it was in the first half! Now that interest rates are skyrocketing, it means that we are close to an end of consumer credit, for only the biggest can afford to borrow. Something ominous is imminent!

We face a hyperinflationary period of stagflation. This is when you have inflation (of the currency, with concomitant high prices) and yet stagnation of production due to the cost of money, joblessness, etc. Inflation with the gross national product being down is leading us to a hyperinflation depression.

1929 was a deflationary depression (no money created—presses stopped). This will be a price-explosion and money-explosion type of correction. Lack of money (deflation) causes a depression over-night. The opposite takes more time as it eats into the purchasing power of the dollar. It takes time to in-flate a nation into depression, but it is real nonetheless. And the correction will seem so much worse than in 1929-33, for prices will have reached such an all-time high and so many paper millionaires will be affected. Savings will be wiped out in the pro-cess of keeping up with inflation in order to just live. People will not be spending their money on pleasure during the last months of this period. They will need to sell things in order to eat properly, for the value of their paper money will lessen to such an extent that it will not be worth the paper it is printed on.

When prices reach such ridiculous heights that you have to have huge amounts of dollars to buy things with, and yet many people are out of work, the end will come.

If the government has to create inflation to meet its commitments, then we could have a trillion-dollar government budget by 1984. That calls for adding about 80 billion dollars to the national budget each year. Add to this inflation the fact of higher and higher interest rates cutting consumer demand for money to compensate for government demand for money, and you have trouble spelled out loud and clear.

If 20 percent interest rates put over 600,000 people out of work in 1979-80, then 25 percent interest rates will do the same or more in 1982-83. Thirty percent rates might close most of the nation's industries. (We have already seen 21½ percent interest rates.)

Inasmuch as so many dollars find themselves overseas, the U.S. has exported its inflation to the nations of the Western world. (There are more dollars overseas than here.)

The dollar as the world's reserve currency (the purchasing unit used to buy world products) has been and is being used widely in spite of its declining purchasing power on the world scene. But overseas there is much discontent with U.S. inflation rates and much talk about turning to gold (or some other currency) or else creating another international monetary unit, such as ECU (European Currency Unit).

There is much talk in European financial and political circles of replacing the dollar soon with one of their own creations, as in the case of ECU. But they may not have to replace it, for if something doesn't happen soon, it may kill itself, unless President Reagan can stop the killer pace of decline.

Let us also keep in mind that interest rates must soar just as inflation in order to keep up with the declining power of the dollar.

For example, an overseas investor with several millions or billions of petrodollars in a bank here must be aghast at the rate his dollars are going down in purchasing power because of U.S. inflation.

He wants greater interest paid him in order to compensate for the decline in the dollar's value, and thus the rates stay higher and higher in order to keep up with inflation.

ARE WE SEEING THE SIGNS OF THE END NOW?

What are the signs?

1. HIGHER RATES OF INTEREST TO MATCH INFLATION COSTS.
2. SOME PRICES WAY UP, SOME DROPPING (as in real estate).
3. JOBLESSNESS INCREASING.
4. INCOME SLIPPING DRASTICALLY FOR CONSUMERS VIA INFLATION.
5. SAVINGS DRAINED.
6. CREDIT BUYING REACHING LIMIT.
7. BANK CREDIT CARDS COSTING MUCH MORE.
8. CONSUMERS REACHING THE END OF CREDIT-BUYING ABILITY.
9. ONLY COSMETIC CUTS IN GOVERNMENT SPENDING—NOTHING GREAT.
10. GOVERNMENT SPENDING (BUDGETS) UP MORE NEXT YEAR.
11. OVERSEAS DOLLAR HOLDERS LOSING CONFIDENCE.

If the Carter Administration had been reelected in 1979 to a second term, I feel safe in saying that we would not have lasted out two years before the correction would have come, due to overseas lack of faith in our system and economic condition. External affairs via dollar dumping would have done it.

Now that President Reagan and his new cabinet are in office, fighting, working, talking, and acting differently, overseas confidence is up, waiting to see what is going to happen.

Now the correction will not be precipitated by overseas investors and holders of dollars (apart from a possible Arab oil embargo). Thus it will take longer under Reagan than under the Carter economists, working with the big bankers and the Fed.

We have gained a reprieve for maybe two additional years. This means that during the next four years we should all get ready!

It remains to be seen how effectively the Trilateral Commission and David Rockefeller's Council on Foreign Relations can move into the power structure of the Reagan forces and cabinet.

Those who are bent on a one-world global government will try to gain entrance, and some undoubtedly already have.

Positions of power, if they are gained by them, will push us further down the road to ruin and into the arms of the leaders of the new international "government for the benefit of all mankind."

There are shadow forces at work in every major nation, all pushing toward this one goal.

The Soviet Communists want this one-world government for themselves, and little by little they are attempting to cover the globe with their influence and power, either politically or militarily.

The Chinese Communists also want it for themselves, and they see themselves growing rapidly in every area, hoping that the Soviets will die in battle somewhere with the Western superpowers, thereby leaving the world for the Chinese to control through Communism.

Then we have the groups who are attempting to control the world through the power of money, as opposed to the power of the gun.

They too are vying for power against one another as well as against the governments they wish to conquer and control someday soon.

Both Canada and the United States, as well as other nations, have powerful insiders in many branches of government and business that are forces of a shadow government that wields such tremendous financial power that it can take us into one-world government soon.

The global managers want to create monetary

situations, military confrontations, major energy shortages, food shortages, and any kind of emergency possible to bring this nation and others to their knees in obedience to their demands for global government.

The biggest tool they have in their hands is money creation: expansion, contraction, recessions, prosperity, building of debt structures, and the final collapse of the pyramid of debt which they are now creating in the U.S., Canada, and other nations.

They love consumer debt and government debt, and they love to create situations for expansion of business so that when business is expanding and increasing the volume trade, they change the money availability, call in loans, produce economic disorder, change reserve rates, and curtail business while they themselves have sold short in the stock market prior to these cataclysmic creations, thereby making much money.

These are the entrenched and seemingly insurmountable forces that the new Reagan powers will have to combat.

FACT 29—WHEN THE FEDERAL RESERVE INCREASES THE MONEY SUPPLY BY LOWERING THE RESERVE REQUIREMENTS, ALL THE NEW MONEY AVAILABLE FOR BUSINESS IS CREATED BY THE COMMERCIAL BANKS THROUGH THEIR LENDING AND INVESTING ACTIVITY.

This is what was originally intended by Congress in 1935 in enabling the banking establishment to make money as a private enterprise itself and to make money available for business purposes in their localities.

But as the Fed lessens reserve requirements arbitrarily, it causes too much money to be created, thus causing inflation, which is reflected in rising prices for the public.

The Fed must therefore be careful in its allowances of reserve requirements for the commercial banks.

On the other side of the coin, the Fed can increase reserve requirements for the commercial banks, and if done injuriously, the Fed causes the commercial banks to have little or no new money to loan out. In some cases the Fed has forced local commercial banks to call in loans in order to get reserves back in order, to be able to comply with new reserve requirements.

This puts the businesses in the community at a great disadvantage. Businessmen must scramble to pay back loans when they are on call from the local bank. This has often meant bankruptcy to the businessman as the local bank was forced by the Fed to cut off loans and pull in loans.

Inasmuch as the Federal Reserve System is so controlled by the international bankers and global one-worlders, you can easily understand how they in their own good time can pull the rug out from underneath U.S. industry, business, and commerce by simply controlling the interest rates at which business borrows, as well as the reserve requirements for the creation of money.

Higher reserve requirements for the commercial banks of the nation mean tighter money and thus less money for business. That means less employment, less productivity, and higher prices for the products already produced. It means a reduced gross national productivity.

This could happen simultaneously throughout several Western nations at the same time, precipitating a crash of democracies and the creation of a socialistic state.

In the aftermath of a rash of international bankruptcies, the would-be global managers, who just happen to be giant bankers of a multinational nature, can step in and say, "We told you this was going to happen. You have not controlled your money supply and interest rates and have caused your own downfall. With your sincere cooperation we will endeavor to put you back together again."

It will appear that they are doing us a phenomenal favor, and what will be more surprising to some people is that they will already have the banking computerization to bring about world banking.

World banking will be the international bankers' previously arranged computerized control for those banking transactions which the Western nations will need.

Their "favor" to us will be the complete unification of the Central banks of the Western world. Instead of several central banks we will have a world bank run totally by them, primarily for their interests, and with the complete socialization of the Western nations as the end goal of their government dominations.

FACT 30—WHEN THE FEDERAL RESERVE BOARD SETS THE DISCOUNT RATE AND THE REDISCOUNT RATE MONTHLY OR MORE OFTEN, IT DETERMINES THE AMOUNT OF MONEY THAT LOCAL BANKS CAN LOAN OUT BY THE RATE OF INTEREST WHICH THE FED CHARGES THE LOCAL BANKS TO BUY THEIR ELIGIBLE PAPER.

Would you trust 12 men with the nation's business expansion or contraction monthly? When they set the rate of interest at which they buy eligible paper from local and domestic banks of the nation, they determine what the discount rate will be for that period of time.

Originally the local bank would sell eligible paper at a discount rate to the Federal Reserve Bank in its area. This is really reselling to the Federal Reserve a commercial bank's loan agreements with a customer at a price actually less than the bank loaned the customer. How much less is governed by the discount rate. (The eligible paper was loans made to farmers, merchants, and other businessmen in the community.)

The Federal Reserve Board determines this policy for banks of the nation. A higher interest rate for discounted paper means less selling and thus less money for the commercial banks. It also means a higher rate of interest charged local consumers.

By watching the Federal Reserve Board's actions concerning the discount rate, and by knowing the amounts of money to be created as determined by the Open Market Committee, international bankers can determine what a good price would be for their money nationally and internationally.

As the money supply and interest (discount) rate is watched by the international money barons, they set their prime rate accordingly. If money is tight (illiquidity) they set rates higher.

This is usually the principle, but at times the international bankers set their rate of interest for the prime at whatever they wish, disregarding the needs of the nation or even the actions of the government.

However, most of the time the actions of the international bankers coincide with the actions of the Federal Reserve Board in the setting of reverse requirements for commercial banks and in the Open Market Committee's actions in determining the money supply by the buying and selling of government securities.

Thus too much power resides in the minds and votes of the 12 men who control the monetary policies of the United States of America.

FACT 31—IF PRESIDENT REAGAN AND HIS CABINET INITIATE LEGISLATIVE CHANGES IN THESE POWER CENTERS AND BRING ABOUT GREATER PUBLIC CONTROL OF THE MONEY SUPPLY AND INTEREST RATES, WE WILL SEE A MUCH MORE STABLE ECONOMY, A MARKED IMPROVEMENT IN THE STOCK MARKET, STEADY GROWTH IN THE AREA OF PRECIOUS METALS, A STRONG DOLLAR, AND GREATER OVERSEAS CONFIDENCE IN THE U.S. ECONOMY.

There is now hope for recovery in the general trends of business in the United States and Canada because of men in Washington who say they are for less government regulations and more free enterprise again.

There is a light at the end of the tunnel, but it remains to be seen whether this was just election rhetoric or will become reality in the days ahead. They have the power to bring about changes that can make this nation as great as it ever was.

But are we placing too much trust in the hands of mere men? Time will soon tell.

There are certain things that President Reagan can do to change things for the good again in America and for her neighbors who trade with her.

But there are also tragic potentials for ill that President Reagan and his able cabinet may not be able to change.

An oil embargo or an oil war would quite possibly

be two of the life-changing events that our new President may not be able to avoid. Either of these two great possibilities could plunge our nation into a bust period during which we would suffer depression as a result of no energy from the Middle East. That would be decisive in collapsing the stock market and plunging the knife into the jugular vein of American industry and business.

Canada would follow, since so much of what the Canadians work at is regulated by the American business owners of industry and commerce in Canada.

What happens south of the Canadian border will certainly happen north of the border, except for two good things that Canadians have going for them—large deposits of available oil and gas, and large reserves of vital minerals. The U.S. has run short of all three of these. Much American oil and gas is currently untapped because of environmental restrictions or oil companies' lack of aggressiveness in getting it. Less means more, you know: less oil means more money for those who have it. Less gas means more money for those who are selling it. Too much of any product lessens its price and thus its stock-market value.

Prior to the Reagan Administration and their plans for the development of oil reserves and gas deposits from the Alaskan slopes to the outer shelves in oceans, etc., we had limited development and thus limited energy along with higher and higher costs paid by the consumers. Unbelievably atrocious profits have been made by the owners of the oil companies. Less means more.

With a highly probable one-term President on our hands in America, we could possibly get the best this man has to offer for the good of the nation. President

Reagan does not have to please anybody to get back into office. He is not obligated to the powerful and wealthy lobbyists (as far as we know).

His only obligation is to go down in history as the President who benefited the people by pushing legislation to help Americans live and produce well.

When the people live well, the government lives well too. More profits come from better business. More profits mean higher taxes as income for the government. One hand feeds the other without inflation, excessively heavy taxation, or burdensome bond-selling by the government to raise the elevated budget.

President Reagan may not lessen the budget as it is now, but he can keep it from increasing tremendously, as it did under his predecessor. (The budget doubled under Carter.)

FACT 32—IT IS EXTREMELY IMPORTANT THAT THE COUNTRY HAVE JUST THE RIGHT AMOUNT OF MONEY AVAILABLE FOR GENERAL BUSINESS.

If we haven't learned anything in the last 200 years about money creation and the right amount of money supply for the nation, then we deserve to die economically in a coming depression.

And if the international bankers who control the money supply and determine the interest rates for this country are so stupid about money as they appear to be by virtue of their ridiculous monetary decisions, then they deserve to be completely replaced. This is a portion of my last chapter on the change that could save this nation.

Suffice it to say that there are those who know exactly what the right amount of money is, and how important that is to the nation as its vital lifeblood.

Some know and cannot seem to do anything about it, for powerful forces sweep their statements and plans under the legislative table in Washington.

The others who know are the ones perpetrating the global government plot on the world.

They know how important the right amount of money to run business is to the country. But they purposely disrupt the amounts, dam up the flow with high interest rates, and constrict the flow to business, while using the flow to increase their own holdings of bonds and interest-rate incomes, and using other subtle means to increase their holdings. They are getting rich at the nation's expense.

The nation is being raped by the money creators, who are privately and consistently reaping the best of the land while innocent people work, slave, and suffer for them.

What is the right amount of money? Well, inasmuch as what oil is to machinery, money is to business, it is correct to say that you can underoil or overoil the machinery.

This is the difference between deflation and inflation of the currency.

Deflation is what happened in 1929. The Federal Reserve System arbitrarily pulled the plug and stopped the presses, so to speak, thereby underoiling the machinery of the general marketplace of the nation. There was not enough money to go around. Deflation of the currency is worse than inflation because it imperils a nation immediately.

Deflation comes via several sources but has only one consequence. The consequence, regardless of how it happens and comes about, is always the depression of the country to the extent of the deflation of the currency.

For example, in 1929 and the 1930's the money supply was lessened so terribly that millions of people were put out of work. Businessmen could not borrow money or get money in any way. The local commercial banks of the community had their money supply dry up. Why? Because the Federal Reserve System stopped the creation of money to the extent that they bankrupted the country into a solid depression and kept on doing it for years.

In the recent recession of 1979 and 1980, when interest rates went to 20 percent and inflation did the same, it was the Fed and the megabanks to blame again. Had they continued they would have plunged the nation into depression again. For some reason they stopped just in time—June 1980.

Deflation can come because of high interest rates or through printing and creating less money. The latter takes place as the Fed demands greater reserves in commercial banks and thus controls the fractional reserve system, thereby providing less money for all.

We had inflation with deflation at the same time, however. While the Fed was increasing the money supply for their own use and for the government expansion of budget under Carter, that was inflation for the nation. But they imposed high interest rates (the highest ever known) on general businesses, thereby creating deflation of the currency in a sense for business purposes and at the same time inflation of the currency for government usage.

Inflation with stagnation resulted. That pushed prices up higher than ever. When you have less production accompanying an increasing money supply (inflation), you have major problems.

No one can tell those who understand this kind of economics (macroeconomics) that they don't know what they are doing. They know very well what causes recessions and depressions and prosperity.

The only way they can be stopped is to change the power of interest-rate controls to a public nonbanking body of businessmen whose interests are national interests and not just banking interests.

This committee of the future must not have bankers controlling it in any way. They can and should advise, but not control. The voting power which determines interest rates and the reserve requirements for banks should be done by independent business economists who serve the interests of all members of the national community—men who are loyal to the Constitution of the United States.

It can be done, but it will take an act of Congress to get it done. Will it happen? It might.

Then and only then will interest rates and the money supply be in keeping with what the machinery of the nation needs. Whether that is a 2 percent or 5 percent increase in the money supply monthly would be determined by honest men, sincerely interested in and possessing knowledge of the gross national product of the nation and its monetary demands.

They would study and know how much oil is needed to keep the economic machinery running smoothly.

There need be no ups and downs of a drastic nature in the money supply and interest rates.

The new President of the United States has the will and the power in his hands, with a solid Senate behind him, to change this now.

It can be explained very simply to the people of the nation in one television broadcast and one printing in all newspapers as an explanation of why we have ups and downs and how this can be changed by changing *two committees*. We do not even have to nationalize the Federal Reserve System. But we must revoke the powers invested in the self-seeking international bankers by Theodore Roosevelt in the 1930's. 1935 caused all this, but we can end it if we want to.

When the Federal Open Market Committee and the Federal Reserve Board are filled with men and women who serve this country and not the bankers, this nation's economy will change almost overnight to one of phenomenal prosperity and greatness.

FACT 33—IF THE FEDERAL RESERVE BOARD AND THE OPEN-MARKET COMMITTEE ARE NOT CHANGED WE WILL ALL SUFFER DEPRESSION IN THIS NATION IN THE DECADE OF THE 80's AND SO WILL CANADA AND OTHER NATIONS OF THE WESTERN WORLD.

Other nations will be affected drastically because of their involvement with the dollar. And if the dollar goes down the economic drain of depression, so will the values and equities of other Western nations.

Keep in mind that we are a great trading partner for Japan, West Germany, and the whole of the United Kingdom, to say nothing of the Common Market itself.

Canada will fail economically and in their monetary system, as she is so intricately tied to the U.S. economy.

In a depression, even the demand for Canadian gas, oil, and minerals would be down from their chief buyer, the U.S. The Canadian economy will unquestionably go the way of the United States economy. (Over 60 percent of Canada's businesses and over 70 percent of its oil are owned by American parent corporations.)

Without a change now by the Reagan Administration, there will never be a change in the macroeconomic structure of the United States and

Canada, and thus we will all suffer inestimably.

But with a predominantly pro-administration Senate and also with strong backing in the House of Representatives (though not a majority of Republicans), the President and his Cabinet of experienced men could keep this nation out of the one-world government plan.

FACT 34—THE FEDERAL RESERVE SYSTEM WAS ORIGINALLY ESTABLISHED TO PRECLUDE DEPRESSIONS AND RECESSIONS. IT WAS ESTABLISHED TO FACILITATE INTERSTATE BANKING AND NATIONAL ECONOMIC GROWTH.

Prior to the establishment of the Fed we had states creating money, cashing checks, and doing whatever they could do on a local level to facilitate the growth of our gross national product.

In the harvest seasons there were great demands on local banks for cash. This upset normal banking procedures at the time in rural communities, and at first it caused great banking panics if a number of farmers tried to collect their funds but the banks (operating on the fractional reserve system locally) were not able to fulfill these demands.

Frequently other banks were called on from the cities to help out in this situation. By this means they avoided bankruptcies, etc. But great confusion came at these periods. Great awkwardness was overcome by the establishment of the Fed in the interstate cashing of checks. (Sometimes a person or corporation had to wait weeks to get the money for the checks deposited. And one bank might not honor the money or check from another bank.)

By allowing the bankers to produce the Fed, and with congressional blessings upon it at last (after the banking panic of 1907, which was manufactured to spur Congress into action to produce the Fed), the Fed could eliminate check-cashing problems, and by holding reserves for the banks at the 12 regional Federal Reserve Banks, each community could function financially with greater stability.

Original state banks were more of nonsystem than systematic banking organization. They were loosely connected and they fought bitterly, as they still do to get depositors in their communities.

Even check uniformity (with respect to size, appearance, and types of paper) was established by the Fed for the banking communities of America.

With the establishment of the Central Bank in 1913, the mobilization of reserves was a great asset for all banking. Now the assets of banks were held as reserve accounts in the local Federal Reserve Bank which served each area. Instead of taking from the funds of city banks nearby in the harvest period, allocations were made by the Fed banks for the rural banks at the time of harvest, when cash demands were greatest by farmers.

When a member bank was in trouble due to local demands for funds, or had overextended itself in credit (by not keeping to the ideals of the fractional reserve percentages), or had any other kind of trouble that a bank might run into, the Fed was there to help.

The original idea for a central bank was not all bad. It brought some good things for America, as well as some bad things.

There is no question that this nation (as any nation) needs a central bank. It would serve no practical purpose to destroy the Central Bank now. But it would serve American interests for Congress to closely scrutinize the powers of the Fed and to recognize it in keeping with the Constitution of the United States and in line with what the founding fathers had in mind.

FACT 35—DURING THE 1800's AND EARLY 1900's, AMERICANS WANTED FINANCIAL POWERS AND BANKING INFLUENCE TAKEN OUT OF NEW YORK. THUS THE FED WAS CREATED TO DECENTRALIZE BANKING AS WELL AS CENTRALIZE AUTHORITY FOR IT, WITH THE GOVERNMENT IN CONTROL.

When the legislation was passed (and various stories are told about the deviousness of the parties involved in promoting it), Congress would not allow the Fed to have concentrated money-creating powers in one area, not even Washington, D.C., and certainly not New York.

They felt that in setting up 12 separate and competing banks of the Federal Reserve System around the country, with each bank having the power to hold its own reserves and create the money necessary for each community or general area of it, the nation would be better served in a monetary sense. Congress was right, but this was foiled in 1933 and 1935.

International banking interests were winning what they wanted, but *very slowly*. We did not have ignorant men in Congress. Many knew what had gone on in Europe in the international banking communities of the nations there, and they did not want a central authority here that was independent of Congress and of government scrutiny.

The 12 regional areas worked well for a time. But the powers granted by Congress to the bankers was not enough for them. They wanted a central authority in one place.

But banking officials around the nation did not want a central bank—that is, those who understood the implications. (There are many bankers today, who do not understand the powers of the Fed and the unimaginable powers of the Open Market Committee.) Those who were in the know liked things basically as they were. But forces were at work in Europe, the United States, and Canada to produce a central bank, as England and other nations of Europe had under the jurisdiction and powers of the Rothschilds.

They would not stop at anything to set it up! There were slight depressions (more serious than a recession) in 1921, and then came a big one. It came in order to bring about the one central authority that we have today.

The Federal Reserve System decided to reduce the money flow by one-third from 1929 to 1933. *One-third of the money supply was cut off!*

This was a classic case of the powers of the Federal Reserve System in the creation of deflation (the opposite of what we have now).

There is only one power in the United States that can create *deflation*, and that power resides totally in the Federal Reserve System.

There are two powers that create inflation—the Federal Reserve System and banks.

Today's problem is both. The Fed is happy to oblige the government in its need for money, for the more money the government has created, whether in cash or credit, the more indebted this nation and its consumers are to the Fed.

FACT 36—THE FEDERAL RESERVE SYSTEM (AND ITS COMPONENT PARTS) WAS ESTABLISHED IN 1913 TO PROVIDE A PROPER, HONEST, AND ADEQUATE MONEY SUPPLY FOR THE NATION'S NEEDS.

In producing check-cashing uniformity, in mobilizing reserves on central locations, and in helping ailing banks when needed, the Fed served well. But it was never dreamed in Congress that the Fed would have the power to create shortages, recessions, depressions, mass unemployment, and the suffering this all has brought on.

There have been many times when, as Congressman Wright Patman wrote, "It has become painfully clear that the monetary policy carried out by the Fed was not sufficiently expansionistic to keep the country moving at a rate justified by the increase in the working force and industrial capacity."

It seemed to be and now is again (through another method—higher interest rates) the plan of the Fed to dampen any investment boom this nation might have. Every time things are on the move, with business investment high, and borrowing producing products and manufactured goods which are needed and wanted by all, the Fed throws a major monkey wrench into the machinery of the gross national productivity of this nation.

As soon as the monkey wrench is in the works, the nation goes into recession. Unemployment statistics increase and production is down. Demand is not supplied. Great suffering is endured by millions of people out of work and thousands of businessmen out of work.

This has happened over and over again. *In every decade* since the establishment of the Fed in 1913 there have come severe setbacks just as business was booming for a short while. History is full of the stories of business booms and business busts.

In every case outlined by Congressman Patman it was a Federal-Reserve-System-created shortage of adequate money at the time of the bust.

Interest rates were not so much the tool of the Fed at those times as now. Interest-rate fluctuation has come about as a latter-day tool of the one worlders. More on this shortly.

Shortages in the money supply came at times of national growth. Can a nation have too much growth? Never.

The natural law of supply and demand is the criterion for the growth and development of any nation.

Demand by the consumers puts pressure on business to produce the products which the consumers want and will pay for. Manufacturers rarely create what the nation's people won't buy.

Products that are overproduced one quarter, that go unsold due to overzealousness on the part of the manufacturer, will go into slack production the next quarter, until the producer has sold off most of his unsold inventories. Demand for anything determines its supply and price.

If demand is low, prices will be low for the products in creation. If demand is low, production will slacken. If demand is high, production will be up and prices will be what the consumer will pay and the market will bear. This is also a time when supply-and-demand laws require borrowing from banks by producers and buyers, especially of larger-priced items like houses, cars, appliances, etc.

Banking was set up to facilitate trade and commerce in the nation, not hinder it. The supply of money available to both parties should be adequately measured by the authorities in the banking meetings and should be established in advance for the promotion of the GNP (gross national product). A growing GNP means a successful nation in every way.

One of the many items that killed the Jimmy Carter Administration was the Federal Reserve's insistence on high interest rates during the latter part of 1979 and especially the year of 1980, as they went to the 20 percent mark and higher. This killed the building industry and hurt the automobile industry worse than any time since 1929-1933.

The country had never seen interest rates like these before, and *the new Administration has the power to stop it.* The people of this great nation gave Ronald Reagan a voting mandate to change the order of economic circumstances in this country. They are tired of phenomenal interest rates with which to run businesses. Consumers are fed up with the current expansion of the money supply for government purposes, but with very little of it available for national interests in the private business sector.

Now is the time for America to get back on its feet domestically with a balanced budget, with a low rate of interest for business expansion, and with less government, as Mr. Reagan promised us he believed in.

I believe that he meant it. I also believe that he will honestly try to do his best to change the situation soon.

When the money supply is balanced with lower interest rates, then we will see business expansion, for then and only then can businessmen afford to borrow profitably. We will see unemployment statistics drastically changed, with a fuller employment rate and with more taxes for the government because of business expansion and more people working.

This Administration can change the interest-rate-setting powers and the money supply of the nation for the good of the people once again. Permanent legislation can be passed which determines government-related powers over the money supply and interest rates. It does not take a lawyer, banker, or economist to understand our problems and correct them. It takes concentration, understanding, and compassion for the people, along with political strength and moral courage.

FACT 37—BANKS WERE INTENDED TO BECOME THE INSTRUMENTS OF THE MONEY SUPPLY AND CREDIT, NOT THE MASTERS AND DETERMINING POWERS CONCERNING BUSINESS EXPANSION AND/OR CONTRACTION. BUT THEY HAVE BECOME THE MASTERS OF THE ECONOMY INSTEAD OF WHAT WAS ORIGINALLY INTENDED. WE REFER TO THE FED.

Politicians and bankers have often been at opposite ends of the poles. Politicians who were concerned about the nation, as in the case of several presidents and members of Congress, wanted an adequate supply of money for the nation's business, as well as proper interest rates for these businesses. Bankers who controlled the Fed wanted to control the money supply as they saw fit, and the interest rates as well.

Why the difference? The bankers know that as you change the money supply and reduce business, the prices of certain products rise as production of them decreases. As an example of this today, look at the contraction of stock prices for certain companies that are in dire straits due to terrible increases in the interest rates. They cannot afford to borrow in order to continue business or expand. Their products may go up in price at present rates, even as producers cannot afford to borrow, and thus the market value of that company or group of companies slips terribly. Their stock price and value is way down!

Interest rates put them in this condition. Consumer demand did not do it, nor did the government. The responsibility for the loss is clearly on the shoulders of the megabanks for interest-rate decisions that hurt the nation's businesses, as in the auto and building-construction industries (among many others that are suffering).

Interest rates can affect the value of stocks on the stock market. Anyone knowing what is coming would buy and sell accordingly.

Does it not serve the financial interests of the banking barons and their friends to know what is going to happen to interest rates? Would it not make them richer to know when to sell? They know what will be going down in the next few days from the discussions and decisions of their men in the Open Market Committee. These things do not happen indiscriminately at all. They are planned.

Millionaires and billionaires are made on weekends, as interest rates change late on Fridays. Human nature will never change apart from an act of God. Greed determines so much of what is done behind international banking doors and around their conference tables.

Because of this greed, savings and loan institutions are failing fast. The money they borrow today to offset loans made in the 70's is costing them twice as much to borrow. They are going bankrupt, and mergers are being arranged behind closed doors in emergency sessions.

But many will fail completely with the high interest rates persisting. Millions of dollars will be lost to investors, who are Americans. The handwriting is on the wall.

Why? Because international bankers have always wanted interstate banking. (Federal regulations now prohibit it unless invited by the state.) But when an S & L goes under, why not arrange a "buy-out of debt" for the S & L by a major bank, rather than see the S & L go under?

Thus you have another in a long list of corrupt

reasons and avaricious practices that are maneuvered by the international bankers and that puts them and their powers in the driver's seat as they attempt to take over all states' banking practices, forcing the little banks out of business and bringing about a global network of financial manipulation.

5

Hidden Facts
About Our Government
and the Fed

FACT 38—WHEN THE U.S. GOVERNMENT
NEEDS ADDITIONAL MONEY, AS RECENTLY,
IT PRINTS UP GOVERNMENT SECURITIES,
BONDS, AND T-BILLS FOR SALE ON THE OPEN
MARKET. THE FEDERAL RESERVE BUYS
THESE SECURITIES AND CREATES MONEY
FOR THE GOVERNMENT. THEY EXCHANGE
SECURITIES FOR MONEY.

Other parties, individuals, and banks can buy
government securities as well, and in this way create
money for the government at the time of buying.

It has long been a shock to me that the government
doesn't create its own money instead of securities to
be exchanged for money. Abraham Lincoln printed
money during a portion of the time he was in power
as President, and he saved the nation much money at
the time.

Governments that print securities and sell them
have been told that they haven't got the sense to control money and create money, and that this should be
left to the experts—who are now throwing the nation
into an economic tailspin with interest rates and the
money supply. I am convinced that the government
could do it better.

As result of creating securities, however, the government plunges itself and the consumers of the nation into trillions of dollars of debt as it borrows from the Federal Reserve System, plus banks and businesses and individuals who buy the government securities.

When the government needs money over and above what the IRS brings in, this is the method of money creation.

The securities are then sold through several (over 21) bond dealers in New York City (the Manhattan Wall Street district).

Prices for the securities (interest the government will have to pay to those purchasing them) is usually determined on Mondays, and the sale of the securities takes place on Tuesdays in the open market.

In this market of bond dealers are traded corporate bonds, government bonds and papers, corporate stock, commodity futures, etc. Major borrowers and lenders from all over the nation exchange their funds there. Not the least of the operations of this market is that through which the United States Treasury borrows the money it needs by issuing government bonds and Treasury bills through the 21 or more bond dealers specializing in this area.

In 1935, after the heat of the Great Depression was slightly subsiding and Congress was still fighting with the resulting problems, legislation was passed creating this bond market in New York City.

The 1935 amendment to the Federal Reserve Act provided that government securities may only be bought and sold in the open market. At that time this consisted of 12 bond dealers in New York, but it has grown to nearly two dozen since.

Congressman Wright Patman describes this procedure. "The Treasury determines each week how much money it will need the following week and notifies the manager of the open market account. All interested parties (buyers) are notified, and bids are made on Monday. Notification is also given the bond dealers, of course. On the following Tuesday of each week the Treasury notifies to whom the bonds will be sold. It is usually to the highest bidders. The nearly two dozen bond dealers (an exclusive club in itself) are in constant contact with each other and know long before Tuesday who got the bid.

"It is here that the Federal Reserve System buys Government Securities for itself,. and by so doing creates reserves required by law to run the money supply of the nation."

The government gets the money it wants.

The Fed gets the reserves it requires in order to create money for the 12 conduit banks of the system throughout the nation.

The other banks can buy government securities too, thus creating reserves for themselves as well as for the Fed.

The banks that are not members of the Fed family are about half of the nation's banks today. More on this later.

As the Fed buys securities in the bond market of Wall Street, it has reserves from which to make money.

The point I make here is that the government could very well have printed the bills in the beginning rather than the bonds, but this was why the international bankers wanted the one central bank set up in all the nations of the world. *The bankers would then control the money supply and the interest rates, and would thereby control the governments, too.*

FACT 39—INSTEAD OF AIDING COMMUNITIES IN WHICH THEY ARE LOCATED, LOCAL COMMERCIAL BANKS OFTEN BUY GOVERNMENT PAPER AND ENLARGE THEIR ON-HAND RESERVES. THIS IS NOT HELPING THE COMMUNITY, BUT IS MERELY A RICHER WAY TO GO FOR THE BANKS. BUT THIS CREATES ILLIQUIDITY IN THE GENERAL MARKETPLACE.

Once again the original idea of banking—that of serving the local community and its economic needs—is thwarted by bankers' greed. They buy government bonds and T-bills and get higher interest than they could from the man on the street or the businessman in the community. It takes little effort to buy T-bills, but it certainly takes careful scrutiny to check out the local business that needs money for expansion or inventory increases.

But the local businessman as he expands and increases his business will help reduce unemployment. The general character economically of his community is helped by his efffort and that of others like him as they are financed by the local banks.

But when local banks buy government paper for higher interest and money-making operations for themselves, the nation is not well served.

FACT 40—WHEN SELLING SECURITIES IN ORDER TO RAISE MONEY, THE GOVERNMENT NEGOTIATES FOR THE RATE OF INTEREST IT IS TO BE CHARGED FOR THE SALE. AS THE GOVERNMENT ANNOUNCES THAT A LARGE SALE IS COMING UP, INTERNATIONAL BANKERS HIKE INTEREST RATES IN ADVANCE. THEN THE NEGOTIATIONS TAKE PLACE. THE GOVERNMENT IS THUS OVERCHARGED INTEREST, ESPECIALLY IF IT HAS A

PUSHOVER NEGOTIATOR DEALING WITH THE EXPERTS.

Why our grown-up government has to operate this way is hard to figure out. After all these years of producing a staggering debt, saddled upon the taxpayers of the nation, one would actually believe that economic maturity and financial common sense would finally prevail. But so far common sense, if it has raised its head in Congress over this matter, has been forced out of the picture by big lobbying interests and the power of the almighty dollar to suppress any antagonism to the megabank bureaucracy.

Imagine our government having to negotiate with the bond brokers in New York City every week to determine the price of money! Can we not get a system more in keeping with the democratic process than this?

FACT 41—BY USING BOND DEALERS AS LEGISLATED BY THE AMENDMENT TO THE FEDERAL RESERVE ACT OF 1935, CONGRESS IN EFFECT SET UP ANOTHER SYSTEM OF UNNECESSARY EXPENSE FOR ITSELF. IT IS ANOTHER HIDDEN FACT OF LIFE THAT COSTS AMERICANS MORE TAXES EVERY YEAR.

When it wishes to get more money for various programs, the government sells Treasury bills and government bonds, as already stated, rather than just print the money for itself, which could be monitored and done for next to nothing compared with what the government is now spending for the process.

The bond dealers in New York are paid a commission by the government to sell it bonds, as well as T-bills to other buyers! So in addition to having to haggle over the price of the secured money, and having to pay the higher and higher interest rates charged by the megabanks and others, the government has to pay the bond dealers this commission in order to sell the bonds in the first place!

This was brought about by powerful lobbying in 1935 and during the Roosevelt Administration. In the height of the Great Depression the congressmen were again conned into this unnecessary procedure for the sale of government securities weekly.

FACT 42—THE AMENDMENT MADE TO THE FEDERAL RESERVE ACT IN 1935 MAKES IT IMPOSSIBLE FOR ONE GOVERNMENT AGENCY TO BUY FROM ANOTHER GOVERNMENT AGENCY. EACH AGENCY WISHING TO ACQUIRE BONDS HAS TO BUY ON THE OPEN MARKET AND PAY TRIBUTE TO THE LACKEYS OF THE MEGABANKS—THEIR BOND DEALERS.

When the Federal Reserve System decided arbitrarily to reduce the flow of money about one-third in the Great Depression, it was done to pressure a weary Congress into decisions not secured in the orginal 1913 arrangement. Many foolish decisions were made in 1933 and 1935 for the Fed System, not the least of which was the creation of the bond dealers.

Why not have a securities board of the government sell government securities without commissions (now paid out of the taxpayers pockets)?

FACT 43—INSTEAD OF THE MEGABANKS SERVING THIS NATION AND ACTING IN A WAY TO MAKE ITS CURRENCY STRONG, WHEN THEY RESTRICT THE FLOW OF MONEY TO THE GENERAL MARKETPLACE THROUGH THE METHODS PREVIOUSLY MENTIONED, WE FIND THEM USING THEIR GREAT CAPITAL TO

BUY FOREIGN SECURITIES AND FOREIGN-EXCHANGE MONEY, MAKING MUCH MONEY FOR THEMSELVES AND OFTEN PUSHING THE VALUE OF OUR CURRENCY DOWNWARD.

Chase Manhattan and other magabanks (through their various offices domestically and abroad) will often buy other nations' money when it is valued lower against ours. The next move is to lower our interest rates, making our dollars cheaper and thus elevating the currency of another nation—strangely, the currency which the megabanks just happened to buy! Such good fortune!

This explains why, when most of the nation is in deep recession, the megabanks come out smelling lika a rose quarterly and annually, with staggering profits announced in the *Wall Street Journal.*

It seems that the two types of financial wizards in this generation that make billions while others are in recession are the megabankers and the oil moguls, both groups of which together in corporate bodies, with interlocking directorates from one group to the other (as I pointed out in my book *The Coming Oil War*).

The eight leading banks of the United States and the seven leading oil companies of the nation are tied completely together at the corporate level. They are all one, in other words, controlling not only banking enterprises but also energy enterprises (and God alone knows how many subsidiary corporations domestically and internationally).

FACT 44—SHORTAGES OF MONEY IN THE NATION HELPED TO CREATE THE FEDERAL RESERVE SYSTEM. NOW THE FEDERAL RESERVE SYSTEM IS AGAIN CREATING SHORTAGES OF MONEY IN THE NATION.

Deflation of the currency, whether in cash or credit, is actually the Fed creating and/or manufacturing less money than the nation needs to operate. As in the case of the oil for the machinery, we need money to keep the wheels of commerce grinding daily. A delicate balance between the gross national productivity and the money supply is absolutely essential to keep the nation producing properly and making substantial progress quarterly.

But though we were promised this by the experts in the propaganda leading the nation to the Federal Reserve Act in 1913, we have not had it.

Time and time again the Fed has elected to slow down the money supply, *not to control inflation* (during the times I speak of now) but to further their own selfish desires.

Curtailment of the money supply affected the value of stocks terribly. Strange that in many cases the elitist bankers and their associates had already sold out on the falling stocks in question! How fortunate for them!

There have been about a dozen periods since the establishment of the Fed in 1913 when the money supply was greatly lacking and thus the industrial growth and commercial operations of the national marketplace were drastically affected.

Simultaneous with this, the megabanks made great profits while the smaller commerical banks (with local interest in mind) did not.

Why have the large banks made billions (as recently as 1981) and the smaller banks have struggled just to stay alive?

The international bankers invested in profitable overseas financial interests. They sold U.S. dollars by the millions on the foreign exchange markets. They invested in gold and silver while it was low and pushed it higher by affecting the precious-metals market with varying interest rates domestically.

While Congress and the nation has been pushed to the legislative wall with bankers' hyperbole over who should control the Central Bank and who shouldn't (Congress), the megabankers turned around and implemented actions on their own, accomplishing their desired ends financially by imposing on the nation's business the very same problems we had before they were put into office.

Now we have inflation with stagnation. We have inflation of currency and yet illiquidity in the private sector. The money is being created in huge amounts weekly, but it is not for the good of private business; it is for the good of the Fed and the government.

Currently the government needs much money, and a great amount of Treasury bills and government bonds are being printed for sale on the open market through the New York City bond dealers. These government securities have a high rate of interest attached to their purchase, as negotiated weekly by the dealers, buyers, and sellers.

FACT 45—THE GREATEST EVIL FOR BUSINESS TODAY ANYWHERE IN THE WORLD IS ILLIQUIDITY. CURRENTLY IT IS ILLIQUIDITY WITH INFLATION.

The Fed officials are completely responsible for what is going on. They are making great amounts of money for their private enterprise by satisying the insatiable lust for money that the big government spenders have. The government is slaking its financial thirst with the largest doses of money ever in American history.

It is counterproductive to have such massive amounts of money created for an institution that never makes any money. The government is the biggest waster of money known to mankind, as President Reagan has been pointing out. He speaks of cutting government waste and thus saving tax dollars and lessening taxes for us all.

If the President can understand the ominous powers and selfish interests of the Fed and the megabanks, he can engage in legislative efforts to control it, since he has a majority of his party in the senate.

President Reagan needs to realize the following points.

1. The Fed is independent from the government in ownership.
2. The Fed is independent from the government in policy, and often its policy runs counter to what the government wishes for the nation.
3. The Fed runs its own program, which is often wrong for the nation (as recently).
4. The Fed is rightly criticized by the building trade officials, as well as by businessmen and laborers, for counterproductive interest rates.
5. The Fed uses its powers of buying government securities to create reserve funds for commercial banks.
6. Commercial banks can buy securities to use as reserves and high-powered money.
7. Interest rates have changed with such volatility as to upset the entire economy of the nation—because of the improper actions of the Fed.
8. Interest rates have risen because of expectations in the rate of inflation, and inflation is a creation of the Fed increasing the money supply to monetize federal government debt.
9. Interest rates are used to keep consumer de-

mand for loans down, so that the Fed can use the increased money supply to buy government securities for higher-interest yields and greater profits.

10. It has been the experience of this nation that when the consumer is allowed to borrow, at reasonable rates of interest, all the money he needs to increase business for the nation, then and only then does the nation enjoy great gross national productivity.

FACT 46—IT SHOULD BE PERFECTLY CLEAR THAT TOO MUCH POWER RESIDES WITHIN THE SECRETIVE DOORS OF THE FEDERAL RESERVE SYSTEM. THUS WE CANNOT RUN A STABLE ECONOMY OR ANTICIPATE ANYTHING BUT ECONOMIC CHAOS UNTIL THIS POWER IS CONTROLLED BY THE PRESIDENT AND CONGRESS OR ELSE CHANGED COMPLETELY.

President Reagan has the potential for this proposed change. We will discuss more of it in the last chapter under what to expect and how to live in the light of it.

We are headed for tragedy or triumph, depending on the new administration. We cannot go another decade with the corruption in government-level economics that we have had recently.

One would think that after all the experiences of 100 years we would have learned about interest rates, reserves, and money-supply explosiveness in the nation. And we *have* learned in the sense that the Fed knows all about what is going on. They know what they are doing, but what they are doing is against the nation, against your better interests, and against the government. Instead, it is in favor of themselves and the future of their coming global enterprise.

FACT 47—NOTHING AFFECTS A NATION FOR GREAT PROSPERITY OR TRAGIC DEPRESSION LIKE THE POWER THAT CONTROLS ITS MONEY SUPPLY AND INTEREST RATES.

There is no power on earth in the affairs of men like the power of money. Whoever controls money and its supply for any nation is the most important power in that nation.

We have allowed men who are *not* elected by the people, who are *not* part of the United States government, to control the most predominantly potent power which the nation possesses.

By calling your attention at this point to the bibliography at the end of the book, I want to emphasize that there are many people who are knowledgeable about the power of money and the interest rates in the world. These established writers can share further with you the inherent dangers of the current Federal Reserve System of the United States.

As you digest what they have written, it will become clear to you that the greatest foe we have is neither the Soviet Union nor Communist China, as formidable as they are. Our greatest foes are those within our own house. They control the power to make or break this nation almost overnight.

They control the power to reduce the nation's business to the rubble of another great depression, before Congress could pass legislation prohibiting it.

I have to believe that as the dollar dies in purchasing power for you and me every week, this is an intended act on their part. They deliberately increase its quantity and thus destroy its inherent quality.

As the quality of the dollar is ruthlessly destroyed by international manipulations, the nations of the world use it less as the world's reserve tender. Finally the day will come when the world will overthrow the dollar and substitute in its place an international world currency, probably backed by gold and recognized by the international bankers. How strange that in their vaults billions of bills of this new currency will already be prepared for mass distribution in the nations, including the United States and Canada!

FACT 48—INTEREST RATES SERVE TWO PURPOSES FOR THE INTERNATIONAL BANKERS: 1) Higher returns on Government securities; 2) Less consumer demand for money.

The reason the Fed gives for high interest rates is to cut inflation. Have you seen this happen?

Did the interest rates of 20 percent cut into the inflation rate to any substantial degree, bringing stability to the economy again? Not at all.

On the contrary, business was in a tailspin, recession deepened, and inflation persisted at double-digit levels.

But the multinational banking corporations made big money. Billions were exchanged, and literally millions were made (if not billions) while the rest of the nation suffered terribly and will continue to do so if things in Washington and New York are not changed by the new Administration and President.

FACT 49—GOVERNMENT DEBT IS A DELIGHT TO CENTRAL BANKS, AND WHEN GOVERNMENT DEBT IS PRECEDED AND ACCOMPANIED BY HIGHER AND HIGHER INTEREST RATES IMPOSED UPON THE SALE OF THE

GOVERNMENT TREASURY BILLS AND BONDS, IT INCREASES THE DEFICIT, INCREASES TAXES, CREATES INFLATION, AND FURTHER STAGNATES THE GENERAL MARKETPLACE OF THE NATION.

High interest rates are said to be cutting inflation and thus helping the nation. In fact they only curtail business expansion, not government expansion. The government sets its budget without any consideration of the interest-rate level at the time. But in order to raise the level of money needed to run the government, it sells government T-bills and bonds. The government is going to get its needed money. The monetary authorities (the Fed) are not going to turn the government down. They want to sell it money at a high rate of interest.

FACT 50—INTEREST RATES HAPPEN TO BE THE NEW TOOL OF THE FEDERAL RESERVE SYSTEM IN THE WORLD TO BRING ABOUT DEPRESSION AND GLOBAL CONQUEST FOR THE MONEY BARONS.

They used deflation of the money supply in other eras (and in other nations) as in 1929 to 1933 in the U.S. and Canada.

Their plan worked, but suddenly and calamitously, and in a world of economic and fiscal ignorance compared with today.

In order to bring about the elitist demand for global government and a global monetary system for the nations, they will be more subtle this time for this will be the all-important one.

Cataclysmic-like deflation would be intercepted by a more intelligent Congress. Congressional economists (or economists working under and with Congressmen) would spot this overnight, and thus legislation could immediately be passed which would increase the money supply to adequate proportions throughout the nation to carry on business.

The general economic depression and the demoralization of the people, (by destroying the purchasing power of the dollar) will have to be more subtle than in 1929.

This time we can have inflation coupled with high interest rates. It will take more time, but it will be so subtle, so carefully timed, and so ingeniously imposed on the the nations involved that it will happen while it looks like the monetary authorities (the Fed) are actually doing everything in their power to stop it.

In the media, it will seem that that the "money experts" are as astonished as we are that unemployment is reaching 20 percent and in some areas 35 percent.

They will be aghast at what is happening to interest rates while we simultaneously have staggering inflation.

No one will have an effective answer—that is, no one with a microphone for a national hearing through the media. The economists on television and radio (and in leading newspapers) will be speechless and confused, and yet probably complimentary toward the Fed for taking such drastic actions to halt this mess. But the mess will not be halted—only increased.

You can look for a planned and programmed depression of our currency and of our gross national productivity.

Are you ready for this? We will deal with it later.

FACT 51—INTEREST RATES AFFECT EVERY POINT OF OUR COMPLEX SOCIETY TODAY,

AND WILL INCREASINGLY DO SO IF THEY ARE ALLOWED TO INCREASE UNCHECKED BY GOVERNMENT OFFICIALS.

We must have economic change or else every segment of our lives will change.

A man cannot afford to buy a new house (or even an older house) for his growing family. Interest rates, and not the price of the house, make the purchase impossible. When you ask him to pay 14 percent interest or more for a 30-year or 40-year mortgage, with a 10 or 20 percent down payment, you knock him right out of the ball park.

Interest rates force inflationary costs upon us in every era of life. Interest rates imposed by the Fed cut the standard of living for every American. Interest rates imposed by the Canadian government and the Bank of Canada do the same for every Canadian reading this book.

Whoever controls interest rates controls the growth of the nation. That growth can be good and prosperous or else terribly disastrous.

FACT 52—CONGRESSMAN PATMAN SAID, "AN ACTIVE MONETARY POLICY PURSUED BY AN AGENCY THAT TAKES ITS OWN SOUNDINGS OF THE ECONOMY AND SUBSEQUENTLY ACTS ON ITS OWN INITIATIVE WITHOUT CONSULTATION IS A COSTLY LUXURY FOR A MODERN ECONOMY."

The Fed can do what it wants to do. "No one seems to understand it, and least of all must not question it, for we all know that money is such a complex subject that only the experts can manage it, control it, and speak wisely about it." That is what they want you to think!

Not only was Congressman Patman totally correct,

but if he were alive today, he would explode. He virtually exploded with interest rates at 2½ and 3 percent. What would the wise Congressman say about the 17 to 22 percent today?

The shame of allowing this to happen! We are a free nation of entrepreneurs—businessmen with expertise—and yet the government has allowed the same powers and authorities to bind us that our forefathers fled from in Europe in order to found this great nation.

They fled from strict monetary control, greed, exhorbitant taxes, and avarice in banking officials to a fresh new world with none of these to affect their vision. They took raw courage and vision, mixed it with blood, sweat, tears, and anguish, and built the greatest nation in the history of the ancient or modern world.

But eventually the enemy got in anyway, and he is now firmly entrenched in the central powerhouse of the nation.

Nineteen individuals sit in discussion and deliberations every three weeks or so on the Open Market Committee to recommend the amount of the money supply, which affects the interest rates and every facet of life in the nation (around the world, in some cases).

Of these nineteen, only five are supposedly independent members appointed by the President. Twelve are the seven members of the Federal Reserve Board, also appointed by the President, and five more are selected heads of the Federal Reserve Banks of the nation.

Twelve members are connected with the Federal Reserve System. Twelve members, along with the other five, take their own soundings of the economy of the nation and help to finalize decisions affecting the lives of 230 million people plus many thousands of businesses.

Is it not possible that these decision-makers would follow policies that are self-serving? Would it be contrary to all teachings about the human heart to believe that they would not make decisions favoring their own financial positions?

FACT 53—CENTRAL BANKS, AS WORLDWIDE EXPERIENCE INDICATES, FOLLOW A SELF-SERVING POLICY OF HIGH INTEREST RATES WHENEVER POSSIBLE.

Many nations have had the same experience, to some extent, that we are experiencing now.

It had to come to us, even though we were considered one of the most financially stable of all nations and possessing some of the greatest economic brains of the world.

It came slowly, subtly, and in sinister form, but it is here.

If the Congress under President Reagan does nothing about this power given to the hands of private individuals, bringing them vast fortunes of wealth annually, then this nation is doomed to economic disaster, to total depression greater than in 1928-33.

My specific predictions will come later in this book, but suffice it to say here that trouble is brewing, the likes of which we have never seen in this or any other nation in modern times (except possibly for Uganda).

People do not have the patience with government (or with one another) that our fathers had even a generation ago. Patience is gone, and character is not what it was. Drugs, alcohol, and the general degeneracy of our life (as manifested in the drug generation, in the dishonesty of business, and in the increase of crime) indicates that humans are not by and large the same wholesome lot that our parents and grandparents were. We possess less honesty, character, and perfection in everything.

Quality has been sacrificed on the altars of passion, lust, greed, power, fun, and pleasure. Satisfaction of the mind, the development of the soul, and the suppression of the appetites of the body that characterized North America is not very evident any longer.

Crime is running at an all-time high. Literacy is lower, with illiteracy and ignorance filling the minds of many high-school graduates.

Where is the sweat that produced big businesses and the honest grocer around the corner?

Some of this is still to be found, but it is evaporating as people see the scoundrels in government taking bribes and White House officials arrested and/or investigated for drugs, illicit affairs, mismanagement of personal finance, etc.

Quality is not a way of life any longer, even in the products we use and the clothes we wear.

Quality is a word seldom used properly today. It is propagandized, butchered, misused, and lied about. Everybody wants it from the other guy but may not be willing to give it himself to others in terms of how hours are spent at work or at home.

"Just getting by" is substituted for excellence in learning, producing, selling products, and living in general.

And this quality of life we are discussing here goes deep into character. Quality is missing, but conniving is in.

Quality is lost in the industrial world of many products. Automotive corporations recall millions of cars for lack of quality.

Government authorities pounce on food companies for lack of quality in their products.

The country may break its seams wide open when shortages appear, unemployment is staggering, and the government cannot safisfy all the people's needs. Hunger, insolvency, bankruptcy, sickness, and disease, coupled with mental breakdowns, paranoia and psychotic behavior, will cause such a breakdown of society that only the "saviors" will win.

Who are the "saviors"? The elitists who believe in one-world government.

Could all of this happen? Not overnight, in my opinion. But it could certainly happen if President Reagan lost his power politically in Congress.

Congressional confusion has always been extremely evident in financial crunches. American history (and the history of other nations, for that matter) shows that Senators and all members of the House of Representatives, with very few exceptions, have been bereft of economic horse sense when depression struck. No one seems to know the best fiscal course of action.

FACT 54—RESERVE MONEY IS CREATED BY THE FED BY BUYING GOVERNMENT SECURITIES AND BONDS.

In case it has not been clearly stated, the Fed simply "writes a check" and pays the bond dealers for the bonds and T-bills being sold by the government to monetize government debts and perpetuate government programs. The government prints bonds and T-bills, and through negotiations with buyers (through the 21 or more bond companies on Wall Street) sells these securities to buyers, primarily the Fed, megabanks, etc.

It is in this way that the Fed creates reserve money

to loan to member banks to use locally through the 12 conduit banks of the Fed.

If the Fed is the bankers' bank and the government's bank, you can easily see how important it is for the Fed to be able to create reserves (high-powered money) for use in the American system of banking and for the general good of the nation's commerce and trade.

Where does the Fed get the money to buy the securities? Nowhere. It simply writes a check out of nothing to buy them.

That check will be paid to a bond dealer in order to buy the government bond or T-bill. The bond dealer places it in his account.

The Fed creates money as it buys securities to create reserves to be used in the banking system.

It has been granted this power by Congress. It doesn't get the money it uses; it *creates* it by writing the check for the purchase. The Fed is a complete money-making machine.

So the Federal Reserve System is an agency of Congress authorized to create money, out of which it makes much monetary profit!

When the nongovernment bond dealer deposits his check in his bank, let's say for one million dollars of government securities, then the reserves of that bank have increased to that amount and have become high-powered dollars capable of being increased to 12 million dollars (if the fractional reserve system is on a ratio of 12:1, as it is now).

FACT 55—EXPANSION OR CONTRACTION OF THE MONEY SUPPLY OCCURS BY A CHANGE IN RESERVES IN THE FEDERAL RESERVE SYSTEM AND IN COMMERCIAL BANKS.

If the Fed increases its reserves by buying

securities, then the total amount of the money supply is increased to the extent of the increase of reserves.

Or the Fed can change the fractional reserve system and thereby increase the money supply without changing reserves at all.

It merely requires less reserves to be held by a commercial bank. Thus they can increase the fractional increase of money and therefore have more to loan out and more to be paid back, plus interest.

With the reserve requirement decreased, the unchanged level of reserves can support a larger stock of "checkbook" money, and the banks will proceed to employ their excess reserves by making new loans and investments.

At any time they choose, they can change the money supply for the nation. The Federal Reserve either changes the amounts of reserves on hand by buying securities or changes the reserve requirement for commercial banks.

FACT 56—THE FRACTIONAL RESERVE SYSTEM WAS CHANGED IN MARCH 1979 FROM 6:1 TO 12:1 BY PRESIDENT JIMMY CARTER. THE MONETARY CONTROL ACT WAS SIGNED, MAKING THIS POSSIBLE.

It is hard to believe that the monetary control of the United States—the Federal Reserve System, which was set up to keep the country from deflation and inflation—would have the audacity to ask for and get a new fractional reserve requirement percentage.

But they got it—lock, stock, and barrel—under Carter. *It is the most potentially explosive act ever passed since 1913 and 1935, when the Fed came into power and full power.*

The Fed's money-creating power was doubled by this act. The new law was passed by Congress without debate on the new act's long-range economic ramifications.

Prior to this act, the commercial banks could create one dollar for every six dollars they held in reserve as collateral. Now the law allows any commerial bank to use the ratio of 12:1, making increased inflation rates definite for the nation now.

Strangely, the established media have been virtually silent about the new laws and how they will affect the American public.

Imagine the control of the newspapers and electronic media when none of them commented on this inflationary law, but just passed it by!

With congressional passage and President Carter signing into law the new reserve requirements, along with other potent facets of the new monetary act, *we are in for unprecedented inflation in the decade of the 80's. This could be our last decade as a nation of independent, law-abiding, constitutionally governed people!*

FACT 57—WHEN THE FEDERAL RESERVE BUYS AND SELLS GOVERNMENT SECURITIES, IT CAN INCREASE RESERVES (HIGH-POWERED MONEY) OR DECREASE THEM, AS IN THE ACT OF SELLING THEM. THE FED CAN LOAN MONEY TO COMMERCIAL BANKS BASED ON ITS OWN RESERVES, AND THUS THE MONEY CREATION BEGINS.

As the Fed increases reserves by buying through bond dealers, it can pass the new reserve on to the 12 conduit banks, which in turn make it available to commercial banks throughout the country.

This creates high-powered money throughout the system, which is now becoming so dangerously overloaded that those economists who believe we are heading for uncontrollable hyperinflation are not far from being totally right. *We are definitely moving in this direction right now.*

When the government's bonds and T-bills are bringing high interest rates (as imposed by megabanks like Chase Manhattan increasing their prime rates), then commercial banks of the nation (local banks) usually take large amounts of deposited money they have on hand and buy these government-issued securities. They too gain interest on them while using the securities as high-powered money with which to increase their available funds for loaning by the ratio of 12:1. This is inflation of a superlative nature. They get paid by creating inflationary money. It is highly rewarding financially to the bankers on both the federal and local levels, while it is economically debilitating to the nation.

One other important fact under this point is that when a private bank acquires (purchases) a government security, the taxpayer over the years will not only pay the interest on these securities for the amount of years that the securities are outstanding (usually a long time), but if and when the federal debt is ever reduced, the taxpayers will also have to repay the principal amount of these securities!

FACT 58—THE FEDERAL DEBT IS STAGGERING. IF YOU HAD TO PAY IT OFF NOW, IT WOULD COST EVERY MAN, WOMAN, AND CHILD IN THE UNITED STATES $112,000. AND IT IS STILL GROWING.

The latest total at the time of this writing was over one trillion dollars. There are other debts not for public record at this time that would push it over the four-trillion-dollar mark!

How has this happened, and why? Well, when

governments wish to spend money, they always find a welcome mat out at the headquarters for the central bankers. Central bankers do not make money by hoarding money or reserves. They make money by loaning it out with high rates of interest.

When the U.S. government wishes to spend money it has a "friend." The government will never be turned down by the Fed or any private bank. Many people want government securities—from private individuals to insurance companies.

After being led down the garden path to demonitization of the gold in the nation, the government and the Fed have gone on a money-creating spree for over ten years.

Billions of dollars have been created that would never have been thought or dreamed possible 20 or 30 years ago by banking officials or government leaders.

No one dreamed of the degree of inflation that would come as a result of the final blow to the gold standard.

It was years in coming. Banking officials on the megabank level had been pushing for it since 1935. They finally got their way.

FACT 59—ALL BANKS, BOTH STATE AND NATIONAL, MUST JOIN THE FEDERAL RESERVE SYSTEM, AS REQUIRED BY LEGISLATION PASSED BY CONGRESS AND PROMOTED BY THE JIMMY CARTER GROUP.

Jimmy Carter, through Zbigniew Brzezinski, promoted the banking bill which gave the Fed complete control over all banks and savings and loans institutions in the nation, regardless of what their status was or what they desired.

Many of them (over half) had chosen not to be a

member of the Fed, and many had left the Fed. But this new legislation forces them to have part (if not all) of their reserves held by the Fed, an act they do not want.

This increases the power of the Federal Reserve System to what they originally wanted in 1913 but did not get even in 1935 under Roosevelt, though they pushed hard for it.

It has taken so much time—the better part of a century—for the international bankers to get what they really wanted in the United States, which is the key country to monetary control of the world.

Inasmuch as the U.S. dollar is the world's reserve currency (the currency used to buy and sell most of the products of most of the nations of the industrialized free world), control over the dollar's creation, expansion, contraction, and interest rates would be mandatory before a one-world monetary control and government could be established.

They are very close to the original goals of the Illuminati of 1776! How long will it take them now?

FACT 60—THE NEW MONETARY ACT OF 1980 ALLOWS THE FEDERAL RESERVE TO USE ALL KINDS OF FOREIGN ASSETS ON HAND, EITHER AS COLLATERAL, OR AS RESERVES WITH WHICH TO CREATE MUCH MORE MONEY.

Inflation is the way out of our Constitution as far as the megabankers and oil moguls are concerned. They are intent on creating hyperinflation. That will end in a terrible blow-off of monetary steam, and then we will have a full-blown depression, the likes of which this nation has never seen.

This coming depression will be a world-wide depression, due to the international influences and the falling value of the world's reserve currency—the dollar.

When the dollar goes down, watch the economy of the nations go into depression after depression, with the strongest and most independent nations going down last, but going down nevertheless.

Now, as a result of the Carter group pushing and pulling on behalf of these Trilateral Commission goals in the new monetary act, we have the Fed and the commercial banks allowed to use foreign deposits and foreign securities, whether on hand or to be bought for high-powered money reserves.

These foreign assets deposited in the bank or bought by the bank on the open market of the world can now be used as collateral to create more American currency in the U.S. through the ever-expanding system of expanding deposits, as explained in the fractional reserve facts of this book.

FACT 61—CONGRESS, IN MARCH, 1980, IN THE NEW MONETARY ACT, ESTABLISHED AN EXTRAORDINARY POWER IN THE FEDERAL RESERVE BOARD: TO SET RESERVE REQUIREMENTS WHEREVER IT PLEASES FOR RENEWABLE PERIODS OF 180 DAYS.

The Fed pushed this through before Jimmy Carter lost the election. Maybe they knew or felt that he would lose to Ronald Reagan. But in any case, they pushed through this piece of "economic embezzlement on the American assets" without contest in Congress.

Can you fathom it—unparalleled inflation ahead! At will, the Fed can reduce reserve requirements for the expansion of the money supply to zero, if they wish.

From nothing we get nothing, in the final analysis. The groundwork has been laid by the Carter group to foist this upon the citizenry of the United States in the decade of the 80's.

Maybe it didn't matter to them whether Mr. Carter got reelected or not. The major pieces of their economic and political platform were surely in place and/or got in place during his administration, due primarily to the men he surrounded himself with—from the Council on Foreign Relations and the Trilateral Commission. Brace yourself, Americans!

In the former days, monetary problems came about because the Fed saw to it that the money supply and credit supply were curtailed in what we know as deflation. But this new piece of permissive legislation is enough to make the Illuminati members of two centuries ago turn over in delight in their graves. Just think—the Federal Reserve System now has the power to militate against the best interests economically of both the government and the nation's businesses and consumers!

The *new* tool for bankruptcy of the government and the people is the monetary implementation of the zero reserves, in order to satisfy the hungry government fiscal policy and public demand.

But this isn't all. Money can now be created with zero reserves for purchasing overseas securities, bonds, and currencies sensitively balanced against the U.S. dollar. They will be bought with U.S. money, thus creating a greater glut of Eurodollars then we have even now, with over 800 billion dollars in existence throughout the world currently.

Then, while the other nations buy dollars and/or U.S. credit dollars in exchange for their securities and currencies, the international bankers and the Federal Reserve can "dump dollars" and buy ever-increasing currencies and bonds, thereby precipitating a worldwide baptism of U.S. declining dollars.

When the final crunch comes in a hyperinflationary blow-off in the U.S. due to too many billions of U.S. dollars buying less and less nationally and internationally, the buyers will be left with worthless assets (or nearly worthless) while the international playboys in the banking world will hold gold, securities, and other valuable international assets that are increasing in value daily as the dollar dies a horrible agonizing death.

FACT 62—WE ARE GOING TO BE THE NEXT WEIMER REPUBLIC VIA HYPERINFLATION DURING THE EARLY PART OF THE DECADE OF THE 80's.

Perhaps most of you will not recognize the title of Weimer Republic, but you may remember the terribly inflationary bust of Germany in the early 1920's.

It is important to remember this period, for this particular period of terrible inflation in Germany gave rise to the dictator Hitler, as did a similar period in the days of inflation under Chiang Kaishek. (That period produced Mao Tse-tung, the world's most hideous murderer of his own people.)

Could the inflation that is coming to America and her allies in economics and philosophy produce the greatest dictatorship of all?

I believe it will.

In the early 1920's runaway inflation caused the German mark to become almost worthless. To buy a loaf of bread you needed a wheelbarrow filled with marks. Are we the next experiment, and the last one before the ultimate fulfillment of catastrophe? Probably so.

FACT 63—INFLATION IS NOW DOUBLING

EVERY FIVE YEARS. WE CAN EXPECT INFLA-TION TO MORE THAN DOUBLE BY 1986. THIS COULD BE THE PERIOD OF 25 TO 30 PERCENT UNEMPLOYMENT AND 20 TO 30 PERCENT IN-FLATION.

A nation as complex as the U.S. industrially, commercially, etc. probably would not be able to sustain that level of inflation without plunging into the greatest and darkest depression of all American history.

The Consumer Price Index (government statistics) indicates clearly what has happened in the past few years. We have doubled every five years in the inflation rate.

At the end of 1978 we were at 8 percent in broad terms. In 1973 we hit 4.6 percent. Prior to that, in 1968, the nation was at 2.2 percent.

At this rate, by 1982 we could reach 16 percent, and we are already at 13 percent! Give us another five-year period and we could easily reach a 30 percent inflation rate. *That is the disaster period.*

This doubling of the rate of inflation every five years took place before this legislation was passed in 1980. That was during a banking period of 6:1 on the fractional reserve system. That was also at a time when interest rates were very low and easy to live with compared to this terrible period of 20 percent and up.

What is going to happen now—much earlier than five years—inasmuch as this ridiculous law was passed by Congress in March?

Look at the facts since then. We have had 20 percent or more interest rates, and at times over 18 percent increase weekly and monthly in the money supply. This is unprecedented in our history and devastating to the marketplace of the nation.

It seems now that the inflation rate (unless curbed by our new Senate and President) will probably double by 1984 or sooner!

In review, consider these facts:

1. Gold no longer backs the dollar.
2. Gold is no longer used in paying Government debts.
3. Dollar creation is no longer pegged to any disciplining force.
4. Dollar creation (inflation) is growing at a rate of double every five years.
5. New laws have been passed in 1980 enabling the dollar to grow at *twice that rate,* indicating a doubling every 2 to 2½ years.
6. With the new zero-based fractional reserve requirement, we could see economic disaster in less time than that!
7. All this fits in with the long-standing plan to create a one-world new order—global management in the event of an international crisis by the international bankers.
8. A managed crisis is their plan now. The crisis that affects all the people and can produce a global government could not be accomplished and expeditiously through any means as the death of the American dollar.
9. *All the machinery is totally in place today.*

The only question that needs asking is, "Will the President see it, will he be able to stop it?"

The question you should ask yourself is, "What am I going to do if this happens on schedule?" Where are you going to live? How are you going to live? Will you have a job? Will there be food on your table for your family, and money in your pocket?

How will you accomplish all this if the President is

found powerless to stop the tide of events against this nation?

FACT 64—NOW WE HAVE CROSSOVER AC-COUNTS. MONEY LEFT IN CHECKING AC-COUNTS CAN BE AUTOMATICALLY TRANSFERED TO SAVINGS AND INTEREST-BEARING ACCOUNTS (AS OF 1980). THIS REAL-LY MEANS THAT THE INTERNATIONAL AND LOCAL BANKERS CAN USE YOUR CHECKING-ACCOUNT OR DEMAND-ACCOUNT MONEY FOR RESERVE REQUIREMENTS ENABLING THEM TO CREATE FURTHER INFLATION.

Savings accounts are called time deposits, and checking accounts are called demand deposits because you can demand them at any time.

Until recently, checking accounts (demand deposits) could not be used as fractional reserve requirements and thus the international banks and the Fed did not like billions of dollars in banks that were not usable for the creation of more money.

But now, as of the March 1980 legislation, the money you have in transfer accounts enables the money moguls to have more high-powered money.

Whoever put together the package for the Monetary Control Act of March 1980 knew exactly where they were going and what they were doing.

Nothing has been more disruptive of the American system of private enterprise and free enterprise than this.

FACT 65—SAVINGS AND LOANS (THRIFT IN-STITUTIONS) ARE UNDER THE FED NOW, AND THE SAVINGS ACCOUNTS THEY CONTROL BECOME RESERVE REQUIREMENTS AS WELL. AGAIN, A PHENOMENAL AMOUNT OF HIGH-POWERED MONEY HAS JUST COME INTO PLAY.

How long will it take, now that all this money and all these checking accounts, savings-and-loans deposits, etc. are in the hands of the Fed, to bring about a depression?

These powers were unheard of in the United States in 1929, so the bankers created a depression through deflation.

Deflation of the money supply is virtually an overnight depression-causing circumstance. As deflation continued, the depression worsened, with terrible suffering on the part of consumers and everyone except the very rich.

Along with the rich in America were those who understood the value of true wealth and hard money.

Real estate had always been considered a boon, but that proved cataclysmic for it was an illiquid investment. No one would buy your house or land because they did not have the money, unles the rich came along and did so.

The man who was ready for the depression, whether conscious of it coming or not, was the man who kept himself liquid in his assets.

He held gold and silver, with preference to the former, for in a time of lack of work, silver demand is down.

The greatest form of liquid capital has always been gold coins. They are immediately acceptable in any country, state, and store.

People have known for centuries, through every depression and political revolution and war, that gold is the best asset to hold in every kind of political and economic weather.

This is true today, and we will briefly cover the subject later in this book. (I went into detail on gold and silver in my book *How to Survive the Money Crash.*)

FACT 66—AS A ONE-THIRD DECREASE IN THE MONEY SUPPLY PRODUCED DEPRESSION IN 1929, SO A ONE-THIRD INCREASE IN THE MONEY SUPPLY BY 1984 WILL PRODUCE THE HYPERINFLATIONARY DEPRESSION. THAT IS THE STUDIED OPINION OF MANY OF TODAY'S ECONOMISTS AND BEST-SELLING AUTHORS.

For further corroboration of the fact that others believe the same thing about a depression, please read the following outstanding books.

Number one is Douglas R. Casey's book *Crisis Investing*. Casey has written one of the best books on why, how, and when we are going to have the greatest of all depressions. He is knowledgeable, forthright, and honest. Read this book. (Published by 76 Press, P.O. Box 2686, Seal Beach, CA 90740.)

Another excellent book is *The Coming Real Estate Crash*, by John Wesley English and Gray Emerson Cardiff. They are two investment counselors of a professional nature, with two of America's oldest and largest brokerage firms, who tell us about the biggest bust ever! (Published by Warner Books, Inc., 75 Rockefeller Plaza, N.Y., N.Y. 10019.)

One of the finest books, by Jerome Smith, an excellent writer and economist, is *Runaway Inflation*—what causes it, what the government should do, and how to protect yourself. (Published by the Self Counsel Press, Ltd., 306 West 25th St., Vancouver, B.C., Canada, V7N 2G1.)

A booklet from which I got much of my information is a government document titled *A Primer on Money*, by Congressman Wright Patman. It was presented to the Committee on Banking and Currency, House of Representatives. (Subcommittee printing in 1964 for the 88th Congress, 2nd Session.) This book is absolute dynamite!

6

What to Expect Next

What should we expect next? That is the crucial question for all of us. Whether you are Mr. Average American, or a millionaire, or a pauper, you want to know what to expect next.

Millions of Americans make less than $20,000 per year and are watching their incomes decline because of inflation eating into their earnings as they are paid with dollars that buy less and less.

As the Consumer Price Index (inflation rate) rises, their income declines. Yet prices for necessary products continue to rise frighteningly.

Everything from cereal to cars, from gasoline to real estate is climbing as the government goes deeper into debt, placing the money secured by the selling of government securities into the national banking system to be used as high-powered money for inflation.

Hyperbole from Washington's powers in the government indicates that "this is all for the good of the nation." Reinforcing propaganda from the Federal Reserve Board is that we are "pulling out of recession" and "good times are coming" if we will only be patient a little longer.

FACT 67—WATCH FOR THE POWERS OF THE TRILATERAL COMMISSION TO INCREASE SUBTLY DURING THE NEXT TWO YEARS IN SPITE OF PRESIDENT REAGAN NOT BEING A MEMBER OF THEIR INTERNATIONAL ORGANIZATION.

Carter, Mondale, Brzezinski, Vance, Brown, Blumenthal, and Volcker, along with 284 others in Carter's Cabinet and seats of power, have been members of the Trilateral Commission and of the older organization, the Council on Foreign Relations.

More information is coming in on who in the Reagan Cabinet are members of the Trilateral Commission.

FACT 68—WE CAN EXPECT THE GREATEST OF CONTROVERSY AND DEBATE IN CONGRESS (WITH THE NEW ADMINISTRATION PARTICIPATING HEAVILY) OVER THE POWER OF THE FED SYSTEM IN AMERICA AND WHAT IT IS DOING TO THE NATION.

It would be completely contrary to what President Reagan promised in his campaign (and what he is attempting to do since elected) for him to neglect this question of the powers of the Federal Reserve System.

His accompanying economists, plus the men making up the Kemp-Roth economic presentation, know of the powers of the Fed, of the exorbitant interest rates, and of the fatal powers of the enlarged money supply. Milton Friedman has frequently lamented the increase in the money supply and is partly responsible for cutbacks by Margaret Thatcher of England, who follows many of his conservative economic theories.

I look for verbal war over the powers of the Fed—at least I desperately hope for it by the Reagan Presidency and Administration.

This is currently our only hope. If this happens, we can expect—

FACT 69—AN EXPLOSION OF POLITICAL POWER AND MUSCLE IN WASHINGTON SUCH AS HAS NEVER BEEN SEEN IN AMERICA'S HISTORY. IF PRESIDENT REAGAN AND HIS REPUBLICAN SENATE TAKE ON THE SYSTEM CONTROLLED BY THE INTERNATIONAL BANKERS, IT WILL BE THE MOST UNPRECEDENTED POLITICAL ACTION EVER UNDERTAKEN BY A U.S. PRESIDENT SINCE ABRAHAM LINCOLN.

It can happen, and if it does, the news media will be filled with the most superlative propaganda imaginable to be sent to the people of the United States.

You will hear tales of overnight depression coming, of "unlawful powers usurped by Congress and the new Administration," of "one hundred years of history down the drain by the President," and so on. There will be more absolute prevarications told by the opposition than ever before in the history of the nation.

They will attempt to tell the people that it was the politicians that produced every recession and depression thus far, and that if the politicians get further control of the money supply, they will destroy the nation forever. Every conceivable type of lie will be told, for once these facts about the Fed, the money supply, and the interest rate ignite the congressional interest, sparks will fly, investigations will ensue, and the truth could come out of all of it!

FACT 70—IF THE PRESIDENT AND HIS ECONOMISTS CHOOSE NOT TO TACKLE THE PROBLEM, OR FAIL TO ENACT NEW LEGISLATION CURBING OR RESTRAINING THE FEDERAL RESERVE SYSTEM, THEN LOOK FOR ECONOMIC CHAOS, DEPRESSION, AND ANARCHY TO RESULT DURING THE NEXT THREE YEARS.

Economic chaos is already here in embryonic form, but nothing compared with what it is going to be like very soon (unless stopped).

Almost every business you can think of is suffering currently compared with how it was faring three or more years ago—all because of high interest rates curtailing business expansion.

The auto industry is in a terrible slump, and all the support industries to the automotive world are in a depression, inasmuch as their materials are not in demand. The unemployment among the steel industry and supportive tool and die industries is up terribly.

When you have a nationwide disruption of goods and services due to the lack of available money for free enterprise, then you have crime, anarchy, unemployment, spiraling prices for available products, and the virtual overthrow of the government.

FACT 71—WHEN THE MONEY SUPPLY IS CUT BECAUSE OF HIGH INTEREST RATES AND FED BUYING OF GOVERNMENT SECURITIES WITH THE MONEY THAT IS CREATED, THEN AS A RESULT OF ENSUING DISRUPTION OF GOODS AND SERVICES YOU WILL SEE HONEST PEOPLE BECOMING DISHONEST IN ORDER TO

SURVIVE. CRIMINAL STATISTICS WILL RISE OVERNIGHT.

At one time in the history of the United States we had people with strong fiber and character. But with the entrance of crooked politicians, etc. we now have a race of Americans wondering about morality, truth, honesty, and uprightness, because the examples set before them are greatly lacking in these areas. It is evident that we do not, on the whole, have the tolerance, understanding, and self-control that our parents and grandparents possessed. This is the promiscuous generation. This is the undisciplined generation.

Discipline and self-control are rarely taught any longer. We hear a lot about *self-expression* but little about *self-suppression.*

Our children are not taught how to face hardships and the tough times of life. They are appeased, compromised with, and let off from responsibilities. It is easier for a parent to do it himself than to teach his offspring.

This is not producing the hard work, the understanding, and the character that America was first built on. Instead it is producing individuals who are dishonest and believe that it is not wrong to do wrong—it is only wrong when you get caught.

I believe you will see very soon a terrible increase in local crime rates—crime that involves stealing food from refrigerators and freezers, plus groceries that the housewife carries home from the local market. It will very soon not be safe to go shopping alone. People will start arming themselves with protective types of weapons. Many people are doing this right now in various parts of the country.

Already farmers are reporting unusually large thefts of farming machinery usually left in the fields.

But in the days to come the hungry and needy may get it and sell it for food, apart from those stealing it now for drugs and pleasure.

Homes left unattended will be unsafe, as will cars and garages. The safest people may be those living in high-rise buildings where many needy families live!

Nowhere will be safe, but urban spreads will be the worst off. Big cities will see unprecedented theft, crime, and disorder very soon unless this international fiscal thievery is stopped by those with the power and in the know.

FACT 72—ANARCHY IS A WORD DESCRIBING A BREAKDOWN OF RESPECT FOR GOVERNMENT LEADERS AND OFFICIALS ON ALL LEVELS, PLUS A TOTAL DISREGARD FOR THE LAWS OF THE LAND.

This has happened many times before in history when economic ills plagued nations and people. They rose up individually in order to find what they needed—ie., provisions for family needs.

Suddenly you find millions of people looking for help and turning to crime and rebellion. Often in history even local government officials have taken to the same means to supply their own needs.

With a disruption of the money supply, with necessities in terribly short supply, and with the trucks and trains not rolling, the nation will experience a terrible disruption of goods and services vital to its existence.

Anything that a person can do to feed his family he will do, especially if others are doing the same and the circumstances producing anarchy are evident everywhere.

Most law-abiding citizens never dream of breaking the law under ordinary circumstances, but this is a situation that could make them join the rest.

When food is in short supply, jobs are running out fast, fuel for transportation is gone, and civil disorder sets in, it will appear that all hell has broken out locally and nationally.

FACT 73—SPIRALING COSTS OF LIVING FOR GOODS AND SERVICES WILL SHAKE AMERICANS BEFORE THE DEPRESSION ARRIVES.

We can expect phenomenal increases in the general cost of living. With inflation doubling every five years even before the Carter banking legislation of 12:1 on the fractional reserve, we can anticipate inflation to double again in much less than five years from now.

The way money is currently being created, the Federal Reserve System could force President Reagan to preside over another 1929-type depression during his administration, and this would force him into actions that would either cancel the Fed's powers (unlikely during this time of terrible stress) or else enable the Fed to take over even more through the global management powers they have set up in order to fuse us all into one-world government.

Prices could rise terribly within one year. Keep in mind what happened in Germany in 1923! Keep in mind also that the Israelis are already facing over 100 percent annual inflation. South American countries are suffering even more, with 200 percent inflation and more!

You would think that our leaders could see what is happening with such devastating speed. It is not as though it has never happened before. History is replete with illustrations of nations taking this tragic pathway to economic destruction.

As money becomes tighter and tighter through

higher and higher interest rates, and escalating inflation hits with devastating force upon the marketplace of the nation, prices for already-produced goods and services will increase *overnight*.

Shortages will come as prices rise and as money becomes harder to get. As prices rise, production slows. As production slows, unemployment rises very fast.

As unemployment rises, so do crime, suicides, psychotic behavior, and fear in the nation over what might come next.

As prices rise, as unemployment rises, and as consumer goods become scarce, the government will step in and attempt to provide jobs, goods, and services that the private sector of the free-enterprise system cannot provide due to strangulation of the money supply.

But this fuels inflation even further as the Fed supplies the money for the government through the sale and purchase of government securities on the open market at higher and higher and higher rates of interest, to be paid back by more of the same. Because of lack of industrial activity the government will have less income from taxes. Thus it will turn to the creation of more money through bonds and the Fed. This will put the U.S. government in deeper and deeper debt to the Federal Reserve System—exactly what the Fed wants. This will make the government look more responsible for the tragedies of the nation and more vulnerable to ultimate Fed requirements and action, thereby bringing us into global management.

When the government is in the supply business, the nation is sick. The nation will die a quick death (depression) unless the nation in the general marketplace gets some blood (money) and starts its own recovery by building a healthy economic base again.

A nation is only as strong as its gross national productivity. Only by this means can it survive as a free nation, providing services, jobs, and goods for its citizens. When government supplies it all, this leads to socialism. *Socialism leads to dictatorship of all constituents.*

When freedom to produce goods demanded by citizens is gone from the private sector and rests instead in the hands of the money creators and the government, we are at the end of democracy.

You can control a government if you have it in debt to you. That is exactly what is happening now.

Current government borrowing at astronomically high interest rates by the Fed means more government control of Americans and more Fed control of policies. What is even worse it means more control of policies of the government during the time of great depression, when it hits with an impact that will make 1929 look like grammar school compared to this university of hard economists.

A government in debt to its central bank is a government over which many insidious controls can and will be exercised.

FACT 74—WATCH FOR MORE GOVERNMENT BORROWING AND MORE SPENDING FOR THE PEOPLE. THIS MEANS MORE GOVERNMENT POWER OVER THE PEOPLE, WHICH IS THE ROYAL ROAD TO SOCIALISM, WITH ULTIMATE CONTROL GOING TO THE LOANERS OF THE MONEY TO THE GOVERNMENT.

To put it simply, the international bankers have embarked on the greatest cover-up story in history. They have a plan so corrupt and yet so clever that almost everyone believes that what is happening is happening for the good of the nation and of the world.

They are cutting the money supply to the general marketplace by increased interest rates. This in effect does the same as what they accomplished in 1929, when the money supply was cut through deflation, as already explained.

But this time, simultaneous with the lack of liquidity in the private sectors of business, they have created great liquidity for the government of the United States. It is a strange set of circumstances, all caused by the existence of the fractional reserve system, a lack of gold standard, and the government's hunger for money to supply jobs and goods for the nation as it starts to suffer.

The bankers are accomplishing this destruction of our economy and our free-enterprise system in the most treacherous manner possible short of war.

We have two types of socialization going on before our eyes right now.

One is *military* socialization of nations, as in the case of Afghanistan and other nations taken over by the Soviets. The other type is *economic and political* socialization of nations, as in the case of Canada, Sweden, England, Israel, etc.

Military socialization differs in the final analysis from economic and political socialization of nations only in the methods used. The goal is the same in either case—global government for the world.

Therefore, strangulation of our goods and services by higher interest rates plus inflation of the money supply for the use of the governments of the United States and Canada are the two major tools currently being used by the international bankers for their quest of global management.

FACT 75—AS GOVERNMENT BORROWING IN-CREASES, AND DEBT INCREASES, TAXABLE INCOME FOR THE GOVERNMENT BECOMES LESS AND LESS BECAUSE OF ILLIQUIDITY IN THE NATION'S PRIVATE SECTOR. FURTHER BORROWING BY THE GOVERNMENT FEEDS INFLATION AND THUS EVENTUALLY SO MUCH MONEY IS CREATED BY THE FED FOR THE GOVERNMENT TRYING TO WARD OFF DEPRESSION THAT THE MONEY IS HARDLY WORTH THE PAPER IT IS PRINTED ON. THEN COMES THE GREAT DEPRESSION—THE GREATEST OF DEPRESSIONS.

The fact that this has all been planned and set in motion years ago (to be filled when legislation permitted) is beside the point. The heart of the matter is that it appears to be irreconcilably upon us today. Only an act of Congress could change the powers behind interest rates and fiscal spending.

Watch for vastly increased government spending to happen fast. Spending will increase to provide goods and services for the nation's people by the government. This will bring at least two things shortly:

1. Greater government control over what it is subsidizing. This means that government will look over and regulate what it is putting money into. This in itself is a step toward government confiscation and is another road to socialism of the nation's productivity.

2. Greater dependence by the people on the government for its handouts, and thus eventual dependence on the government in the form of total socialization and corruption.

Surely the government will have the legal right to govern, regulate, and control what it is investing billions in. That leads to controls beyond what our nation has experienced thus far. It leads to socialization of the nation's wealth. It means that the international bankers will gain control without firing a shot or shooting a shell at America in war that we could call World War Three.

FACT 76—THE ULTIMATE GOAL OF THE INTERNATIONAL BANKERS IS THE GLOBAL SOCIALIZATION OF THE WORLD. THUS IT IS POSSIBLE THAT WITHOUT WAR AND WITHOUT AN EMBARGO, AMERICA COULD COME TO THAT POINT POLITICALLY. THEY HAVE AT LEAST THESE FOUR TOOLS TO WORK WITH (ALL MAY NOT BE NEEDED): INTEREST RATES, MONEY SUPPLY, OIL EMBARGO, AND WAR. THEY CAN PRECIPITATE A CHAOTIC CONDITION IN NORTH AMERICA (CANADA INCLUDED) THAT WOULD BRING ABOUT CRISIS MANAGEMENT OF THE NATION "FOR THE GOOD OF THE PEOPLE."

We may not have to fight the Soviets. We may not have to fight over oil (though we probably will), if only the international bankers can force a situation involving both nations (with the U.S. as the first tool) into an emergency situation requiring emergency legislation, with political action placing all the people under central government control in order to solve the situation.

In 1979-80 legislation was set up by the Carter people in the White House using Brzezinski and others (who belong to the elite party of socializers) which enables a new board of directors or a new committee with emergency powers to take over the reins of the nation in any emergency.

The media gave little recognition to the White

House memorandums and newly created emergency powers and orders.

It would be a wise study on your part to understand what this sweeping EO (Emergency Order) means to you, your family, your community, and your country.

The new FEMA has been set up and is in orbit with complete powers right now. (FEMA means Federal Emergency Management Agency.)

Unknown to most Americans, former President Carter promulgated a secret program giving him powers to suspend the Constitution and to clamp executive authority on the nation for as long as necessary to "end an emergency."

It would depend on the President's judgment as to what is necessary. All would depend *on his judgment* as to whether this was a "national emergency."

In any "national emergency" these sweeping new powers would enable the President or his appointees to virtually replace the Constitution with FEMA in order to "end an emergency."

Some who helped draft the legislation within the White House call it "the most dangerous internal attack on our system since our very beginning."

It is known as Presidential Review Memorandum 32 and is a major White House directive (PRM 32).

It came about in June 1980 as a "national administrative reorganization project," allegedly designed to help the country deal more efficiently with disasters and mass emergencies.

In sharp contrast to past White House directives, PRM#32 has been hidden from the public under a high level of security classification. It has never been published even in the Federal Register, as is customary for such actions.

Since the Roosevelt era, "executive orders" or

presidential decrees, which require the force of law 15 days after publication in the Federal Register, have been used by the mushrooming bureaucracy to extend its control over every significant element of the private sector of American society.

The worst and most powerful of these was initiated on October 28, 1969, under President Nixon.

Currently the FEMA powers enable the President or his appointees to do the following things, which are most alarming when you consider that this is not a Communist nation, nor a socialistic one yet, nor a dictatorship.

But here are the sweeping powers of FEMA, and who knows who is going to manage these powers in the new administration?

FEMA means that a committee of the President's appointment under his guidance can:

1. Take over all communications media. This includes magazines, papers, radio, TV—everything. (It could mean the termination of free broadcasting as some stations and newspapers sincerely try to objectively present the news. It also includes religious programming.)

2. Seize all sources of power, including electric, nuclear, coal, petroleum, etc.

3. Control all food resources in the nation. This means production, manufacturing, processing, distributing, and retailing.

4. Seize all forms of transportation in the nation—buses, trains, planes, trucks, and perhaps your car.

5. Commandeer all civilians to work under federal supervision.(Sounds like Russia to me. I've been there four times and watched this in action.)

6. Register (for selective service) every man,

woman, and child in the U.S., with military or civil service mandatory.

7. Shift any segment of the population from one location to another as the government sees fit.
8. Take over all farms, ranches, or timberland properties, so as to protect, utilize, and manage them properly.
9. Freeze all wages and prices.
10. Regulate the amount of money you can withdraw from your accounts.

FEMA is in reality, the administrative skeleton of a second government for the people of the United States. Its actions are unprecedented in this republic and are subject to neither congressional consent nor judicial approval.

FACT 77—WE ARE ON THE ROAD TO THE COMPLETE SOCIALIZATION OF NORTH AMERICA AND EUROPE IN THE DECADE OF THE 80's. SOCIALIZATION SEEMS INEVITABLE IN THE BRAINWASHED MINDS OF THE CITIZENRY. BUT IT IS A SYNONYM FOR COMMUNIZING THE INDUSTRIALIZED NATIONS.

We would rather be "dead than red." Most North Americans and Europeans think this way. But the global managers get us thinking about fighting Communism politically and even militarily while they insidiously and treacherously move the nation into a socialized position through money management.

Who cares how we arrive at socialization? Certainly not the elite who are pushing for it internationally.

Call it anything you wish—Communism, capitalism, socialism, free enterprise, autocratic control. The don't care what labels we use for what we have or want as long as the net result is the socialization of the world by the global managers, who will then control production, distribution, wages, prices, banking, and policies in every arena of life and industry, including oil, food, and human management.

FACT 78—INTERNATIONAL BANKERS HAVE FINANCED COMMUNISM AND ENCOURAGED AND FINANCED ITS EXPANSIONISM. AT THE SAME TIME THEY HAVE EXERCISED GREAT CONTROLS OVER CAPITALISM. CHASE MANHATTAN IS THE CHIEF BANK IN COMMUNIST COUNTRIES AND IS THE CHIEF BANK FOR WORLD CAPITALISM.

The international elite believe that through trade, commerce, and technology they can keep their hand on the Communists in spite of their independent wishes for global supremacy (without the bankers). Few Communist leaders understand what is going on. Those that might understand believe that in the end they will win over the bankers and will in the meantime use what is given them to further their own desires of global conquest for Communism.

Communism depends on free trade with the West in order to grow and expand. Look at the wheat, soy beans, lumber, steel, and technolgy (for tires, trucks, cars, planes, and computers) that the West has sold them so cheaply. All of this was and is arranged by the international financiers promoting their own brand of socialism, to the end that they can control even the Russians and Chinese Communists.

Again, it is the power of money and the things that money will buy that brings about this hoped-for control of Communism.

It is true that the Communists will agree to some things just to get the consumer goods they need but cannot produce themselves (along with technology not yet mastered by them).

The Chinese leaders are a perfect example of this attitude now in the 80's. They hate Americans and the so-called democratic way of life here. But they are willing, even glad, to trade with us and make loans with us in order to get what they need to conquer the world.

The elitist bankers know this, but they believe they can control it by controlling the flow of money, credit, and goods to the Communists, thus bringing about a discipline and a correction that will eventually bring all these nations under their control along with the Western nations.

Thus the bankers can control the growth of Communsim by liquidity and illiquidity, the same as they can control the West.

They believe that in a final showdown, moneypower rather than gunpowder will bring about the answer as to who rules the world.

They are balancing their monetary power against the Communists' gunpowder, and it is a sensitive balance of power that could be tipped in either direction if either power is allowed to continue much further into the decade of the 80's.

As the Communists build rapidly, they stand to tip the scales on their own behalf against the powers of the monetary artists. Time is fleeting away. I believe we are going to see big action soon.

As the bankers know, if they do not act with haste now that the Communists are building so fast, they stand to lose much. The Soviets have a large supply of gold and oil, and they could go it alone if they wanted to, now that they have achieved such remarkable goals technologically (with the Western powers' help).

FACT 79—SOCIALISM BRINGS ABOUT COMPLETE POLITICAL CONTROL OF THE NATION, WITH ECONOMIC AND FISCAL CONTROL OF MONETARY AFFAIRS AND MILITARY BACKING TO SUPPORT IT.

The Eastern Slavic countries of the European sector prove this. Look at the problems of Hungary, East Germany, Poland, Czechoslovakia, Estonia, Latvia, Lithuania, etc. if you wish to see socialism at work. There was military intervention, political reestablishment, and monetary control set up in each case.

The Soviets are crushing the will and spirit of the Afghanistan people as best they can by political repression, economic reprisals, and military powers. My hat is off to the brave guerillas fighting them daily. As you look at this military type of socialism you see an example of the price that people have to pay to fight it and live under it.

Consider China under the late Mao for a moment. The CIA has documented that over 100 million Chinese died over a 30-year period while Mao was thrusting Maoism (Communism) upon China's one billion people.

The Cultural Revolution alone took the lives of over 50,000 people, many of whom were the intellectuals of the land, in order to subject it to the "blessings of Communism."

Communism is capitalism in reverse form. They use labor, profit and loss, wages and prices, all for their own aggrandizement.

In true capitalism (as in the free-enterprise sections of the world), labor is used to produce goods that others want, and the law of supply and demand for any product determines the price it will bring. The laborer receives his pay, the manufacturer receives his wholesale price, the retailer gets his part, and the consumer receives his product. Everyone shares in the production of a product in the free-enterprise system.

Not so in Communism. Only the hierarchy get the lion's share of the wealth. They are the ones enjoying

Western meats, products, and machinery, such as automobiles, air conditioning, television sets, and video recording facilities in their chateaus and villas in the Soviet Union. The peasants never see these things.

The elite control wages, prices, profits, ownerships of business, and law. They impose what law they like. There are no referendums or propositions to vote on in the Communist world.

Communism, as you know, confiscates ownership of business for "the equitable distribution of profits to all."

"Equitable distribution of profits to all" means to all the big boys sitting in plush offices in the Kremlin. They are the ones enjoying the big cars, plush offices, advanced technology, expensive foods, and fine clothing that we Americans take for granted every day.

Four times I have been in the Soviet Union. I saw suffering, impoverished living, lack of consumer goods, and disgust everywhere.

They hardly believe that we live like we do. They believe that the reports are just propaganda to cover what repression we really live under, especially minorities.

They believe that we live under great government controls, repression, and difficulty. Try telling a Soviet citizen that you have two cars, a double-car garage, central heating and air-conditioning in your home, and two or more television sets through which you get 8 to 10 channels, and watch the reaction on his unbelieving face.

I tried it. I was met with such a incredulous look that I could only have been considered a liar.

They believe they are better off than we are. They

believe they came to our rescue in World War Two and won it for us!

Doctors' salaries, steel workers' salaries, and all other salaries are set by the government. There is no incentive to work hard and get ahead.

Five million men are in uniform, but not by their own volition. Conscription is mandatory for all and is necessary to preserve the way of life imposed on the impoverished people.

Less than 9 percent of the people are card-carrying Communists. The rest have the system imposed upon them.

FACT 80—FREE ENTERPRISE, WITHOUT GOVERNMENT INTERVENTION, DISTRIBUTED GOODS AND WEALTH AS NEED DEMANDED, BASED ON THE ECONOMIC PRINCIPLE OF SUPPLY AND DEMAND OF A PRODUCT. WEALTH WAS MORE EQUALLY DIVIDED. THE MORE BRILLIANT A MAN WAS, THE MORE ENTERPRISING HIS FIRM BECAME AND THE RICHER HE COULD BE. WEALTH WAS ACHIEVED BY PERSONAL EFFORT, FAMILY EFFORT, AND/OR BUSINESS EXPERTISE.

Under the Communist system the state owns all and controls all. It sets all prices and establishes all salaries and benefits for all employees.

What is the difference between Communism and socialism? We are against Communism in this country, but many people feel that enlarged government and virtual socialism is inevitable for America.

What is the final difference?

Communism is accomplished by war, bloodshed, repression, and torture by secret police. Socialism is accomplished by political maneuverings, monetary chicanery, and fiscal mismanagement. Socialism is complete control of the people—their wealth, their health, their future, and all the profits of the nation—by the "new owners of government."

It is Communism without bloodshed (in most cases). It is the same as Communism as it grows in power over the people, but it is usually accomplished under the guise of "managing a crisis" for the people. What the people do not understand is that the crisis was created by the same people now managing it!

FACT 81—WHEN INTEREST RATES ARE HIGH, OVERSEAS INVESTORS ARE VERY PLEASED AS THEY INVEST IN THE U.S. ESPECIALLY DO HIGH INTEREST RATES ACCOMMODATE THE OPEC NATIONS, WHO HAVE BILLIONS OF U.S. DOLLARS IN PAYMENTS FOR OIL IMPORTED INTO THIS NATION.

The interesting fact is that by changing interest rates and moving them upward at will, the international bankers who hold much of the OPEC world of money in their vaults can make their Arab owners very happy.

The question about this fact is, How often do OPEC members state their threats to remove their large amounts of money from those banks unless interest rates are high for their benefit?

Certainly they benefit by high interest rates, for as their money is used as high-powered money and is loaned out to others, they get a higher rate of return for these large amounts. This makes them happier about leaving their money in the U.S. banks.

There is no question that much interest-rate manipulation in the prime-rate level is done to keep overseas investors' money in U.S. banks for the greedy use of the American international bankers.

But while they are feeding themselves with these

interest rates and making OPEC members happier, they are robbing the American public and ruining the businesses of America. At the same time they are creating massive amounts of inflation by using foreign deposits for money creation and are killing the dollar and its purchasing power domestically.

Too much power resides in the hands of those who act constantly in self-seeking ways. High interest rates only serve to make the rich much richer and the poor and middle class much poorer in every way.

7

Arm Yourself
for Boom or Bust

In every possible way, arm yourself for the immediate days of the 1980's. *They could be the toughest you have ever encountered.*

Consider the facts that are currently facing us.

1. We could have an international depression affecting every single North American within 36 months or less, brought about by staggering interest rates.
2. We could have unbelievable bankruptcies hitting the economic scene of American's way of life within six months.
3. Either of the former could effectively put you out of work and thus out of an income for some time.
4. We could be facing the mighty thrust of the Soviet Union in the coming oil war. Many people would be drafted and bloodshed could be high for both sides.
5. An oil embargo would plunge the nation into the greatest struggle for its existence in its history.
6. Shortages of food could ensue, plus shortages in fuel for heating, cooling, and living.
7. Anarchy could fill the land, with crime in the streets and little or no protection by authorities.

8. We face a social breakdown of morals, principles, and law.

There is much more. But let's leave the gloom for now, with the list as it is.

What can you do to prepare yourself for the foregoing?

FACT 82—PREPARATION FOR YOUR PSYCHOLOGICAL SURVIVAL IS NECESSARY NOW.

"As a man thinketh in his heart, so is he." This simply means that if you are fearful, frightened, and unbelieving in your thinking, you will become just that way in your actions, and thus you will be a failure in the coming days.

In a sense, it is the survival of the fittest, with the fittest being those who prepare themselves for the worst in the best possible ways known to them. Let me show you what I have in mind.

Psychologically, you can prepare yourself by being a positive thinker for today and the near future, when the calamities will come.

Many are breaking down mentally today. They are caving in to the realities of unemployment, shortages, suffering, and hardships already in this nation. The suicide rate has never been higher than now. Nor has the nervous-breakdown rate ever been higher in American History.

Psychiatric institutions are filling up everywhere, in every state, and we cannot build large facilities fast enough to accommodate the mentally collapsed.

Many cannot stand unemployment and bankruptcy—the shame and bewilderment of a lifetime of work at a particular profession or position suddenly ending. They cannot handle their own thoughts, worries, and apprehensions. They cannot bring themselves to believe that things are going to get any better for them. As a matter of record, most believe that things are going to get worse financially and that this life holds no future for them anymore.

Marriages are now breaking up more often over money than over sex.

Husbands are running away, and so are wives (who are also mothers) leaving hopeless situations at home.

Drug addiction is increasing as a way out of reality. Alcoholism offers millions an escape from reality. and alcoholism is on the rise in every state of the nation. Much of this rise in both drugs and drinking is due to economic pressures on a generation that cannot handle "not having what they want."

We have been a nation of "getters." Anything a person realistically wanted in the line of pleasure, things, travel, etc. he could usually achieve. But now people can't get what they want because they are not earning the necessary money any longer, due to high interest rates and inflation.

Many Americans cannot handle what is coming, nor will they be able to contain themselves when they realize fully why this is happening to them.

Preparing yourself psychologically is going to involve the development of inner strength and inner qualities that are there, though perhaps latent and dormant.

Character development is never easy, but this is what we are talking about if you are not going to panic!

Strengthening yourself with the weapons to succeed for the future, you begin with a strong mind.

Worrying now will bring panic later. Being concerned now is wise, but worry and paranoia now are futile and destructive. Worry and fear bring indecision and indecisiveness to your thinking patterns and your future.

Fear will throw you into reverse gear, not forward. It will generate confusion, not clear thinking for proper planning. Fear is a killer and totally demolishes your future as it grows within you. We can all fear what is coming, but we need to make sure our fear is not paralyzing us and our thought patterns.

I honestly fear for what is coming on the human race, but not in a way that paralyzes my planning for it all.

Fear can be a healthy attitude, but only to a point. Without any fear one might walk into the pathway of a car. We could do ridiculous and perhaps even fatal things.

But let your fear of the things that are coming be a fear that produces thinking and planning, because you want to be ready for what you fear. Fear must only take on the form of respect for what is going to happen in the future and the form of concern over what to do in order to be ready.

Fear brings either paralysis or confident planning. If you have arrived at the latter, then you have faith to believe that you can do something about what is going to happen to you and yours.

That is good. Confident planning is what is necessary. In order to have that kind of presence of mind, do not give in to fear that kills.

Refuse to give into confusion, despair, or discouragement over your circumstances. Refuse to believe that there isn't a way out. If you believe there is a way out, there will be!

Faith brings its own solutions as necessities arise. Faith that there is a way out brings ideas, planning, and strength.

Faith rejects fears that are unwarranted and unreasonable. Faith that you can make a way for yourself brings more faith and thus more self-assurance and inner strength.

Fear clogs the channels of pure, constructive thinking with evil influences.

Faith opens the channels of clear, positive thinking, and good ideas come fast.

You can be wiser tomorrow than you are today by faith-thinking and fear-shrinking.

Get alone with your own thoughts and strengths, and draw them out. Outrightly reject confusion, fear, and their companions. *You do not have to think negatively. You can force your mind and your thought patterns into positive thinking.*

Call it a crutch if you like, but I get my strengthening thoughts of faith and I conquer my fears by reading my own personal Bible daily.

It contains psychiatry for today. I read about being "able to do all things." That is great. I read about "nothing being able to conquer me." I need that positive faith-building impetus daily. I read about "be it unto you according to your faith," or "Without fear nothing is possible; with faith everything is possible."

I get strength, inner peace, and preparedness for the future by praying. It unloads the garbage out of my mind and brings in a fresh supply of power, clear thinking, and positive action.

Your church attendance can get you started on these faith-building steps.

Whatever brings you peace of mind and strength of thought, do it. Alcohol, drugs, etc. will only postpone the action of thinking and may even permanently make it impossible.

Get out of town to the mountains and walk through the trees. Get into your jeans and walk through the woods and get away from the pressures of the office and home for the weekend. Fresh air and a change in diet can help you think more clearly.

For some people a trip to the beach and a plunge into a warm ocean surf can help clear the mind and get rid of the mental debris that wears you down so fast.

Ride a horse, go fishing, take out a boat, or walk alone, but get rid of daily pressure. Leave them at home while you head for a change of atmosphere.

Even if you are broke today, you can make it through what is coming by having a clear head to think with. You will think positively and then plan positively.

By keeping your mind strong you are ready psychologically for whatever tomorrow is going to throw at you.

Changes will come. Plan on them. They will not all be for the good at the moment, but you can face them with strength and peace, especially if you get God's help. He cares for you and wants to you know it.

FACT 83—OWNING GOLD COINS WILL BE YOUR GREATEST SOURCE OF ECONOMIC SURVIVAL IN THE COMING DEPRESSION AND CALAMITIES.

This is not a book on gold. There has been much written for and against gold ownership in crisis periods, and I am *much for it.* Please read my latest books containing long chapters jammed with facts on gold that will enlighten you, help you, and enable you to more completely understand the strength of gold now and in past history.

When money collapses in the coming correction of all values related to the dollar, then *whoever owns gold* will come out on top safely and successfully, depending on how much gold he has.

In my books *How to Survive the Money Crash,* and

The Coming Oil War I extol the virtues of gold owner-ship for all. I believe that, as in all depressions and recessions in history, gold will once again supply its owners with all they need for survival during this terrible period and will also provide them with the one great thing they need to become wealthy and successful again—the power of true wealth.

Gold is power because gold is true wealth in that it is truly appreciated and desired by every peron of every race in every continent of the world. There is no earthly power like gold power.

I will not repeat in this book the intrinsic wealth and value of gold and silver, as I did in the other two books mentioned, but I do hope for further expan-sion on your gold thinking and gold portfolio for the future and today as you read both of those books.

Even if gold merely held its current price, and did not increase at all, you would still be buying an unbelievable increase in your wealth as everything else corrects in value downward. If prices go down by only 75 percent, you have multiplied your gold value by 400 percent insofar as purchasing power is concerned. That is almost incredible, but it is true.

Look at it this way. You are a farmer with a bull to sell at today's price of $1000. The depression comes and the bull brings only $250 on the market in the corrected value of dollars.

I come along with gold coins worth $1000 today and at the *same value* in the depression. I can buy on-ly one bull today, but in the depression I can buy four! I have increased my purchasing power by 400 percent in a depression that bought corrections to the tune of only 75 percent. If there is a 90 percent cor-rection in the value of the dollar, I could buy 10 bulls at $100 each with my steady value of $1000 in gold coins.

It is foolish to hold onto anything that will correct downward in the coming depression. It is wise to hold onto anything that will hold steady or increase in value at that calamitous time.

FACT 84—BUYING GOLD TODAY IS EASY. YOU BUY IT AS ANYTHING ELSE—WITH PAPER MONEY IN A GOLD-COIN STORE.

So many people write me and ask how and where to buy gold coins. I do not sell gold in any form, and I recommend that you buy coins in your own community or anywhere you can find through the Yellow Pages of your phone book. I recommend buying South African Krugerrands.

Call first and talk to the dealer about them. It will arm you with much information on how to buy and what to ask for.

The more you buy, the less they cost, and that is better for you. But buy, whether you buy one coin or a hundred!

One $500 coin could go to $2000 or higher! As prices correct, you will see your values go from $500 to possibly $7000 or more in purchasing power in the depression.

Hold onto these coins, and do not sell them for any reason today. Do not get greedy and sell because gold goes to $1000 next month. You did not buy for now. You bought for success and survival in the coming dark hours.

When you buy, always take possession of your own coins, never leaving them for safe storage with anyone but yourself.

The coins usually come in little plastic containers and you can store them anywhere you feel is safe.

Some have placed them in the ice cream in the freezer and left them there for years. Others have

floor safes, and still others buy the burying l
plastic container and bury the coins in the grounu,
where only they could know where they are.

Many people are using safety-deposit boxes in
organizations not connected with banking in any
way. Several major cities have these now.

The point is to buy them, hold them, and tell no one
about your possessing them. This is your emergency
survival kit for economic freedom and quick success
when the crash comes.

FACT 85—HAVE A GETAWAY PLAN MADE AND CHECKED OUT.

Sounds logical—or does it sound ridiculous? Well, if
you consider what can happen in your city, with
many jobless and thousands or millions hungry, it
will appear wise to you to consider getting away
from it all.

Let's say you live in Chicago, Los Angeles, or New
York. All hell breaks loose, with looting, stealing,
fires, frenzy, paranoia, resentment, loss of law and
order, etc. Many people will lose their lives as well as
their homes, autos, and other items of value during
this time of national frenzy. Remember that
Americans have never had to go through anything
like this before.

The major metropolitan areas will be hit hardest
first. The "have-nots" will not be sitting around
smoking, grumbling, and waiting for the government. They will be coming after you and what you
have, regardless of your color, race, and religion.

Where could you go that would be safe for you and
your children and family? There may be two or
three families that will plan this together. That is
good, especially if each can contribute differing
talents for the occasion.

As soon as you can, figure out where you are going and how you are going to get there. Will you use a car, a truck, or a plane? Will it be on the continent itself or abroad?

Would you go to Canada as opposed to anywhere in the U.S.?

Are you going to go in advance and stock your apartment, your cabin, or your winter or summer home with foodstuffs, water, and other provisions? Or do you feel you will know when this is going to happen and will be able to jump the gun on others and get there and buy and stock at that time?

Canada will be safer than the U.S. at this time simply because she has far less population. Canada has only 10 percent of the population of the United States currently and has much land, water, and resources to be used (including oil), and thus will be in a better position to feed her people than the U.S. will be.

A trip to some part of Canada may be your best vacation idea, to look things over and make your plans safe and thorough.

You say you do not have the time or the money to buy a place in Canada that is sufficiently remote to be safe?

Go to a large bookstore and buy several travel books in which hotels, lodges, resorts, and camps are spotted and discussed in length. Some stores have such books on their travel shelves.

In these books you will find listed the names of owners and proprietors of furnished apartments, hotels, cabins, and resorts (ski resorts are excellent), and you can write or call these places and get much information as to what is available.

You don't have to buy anything. You can rent everywhere you go, and everything you need is supplied.

Take a ski resort in British Columbia, for example. You can get a ski lease for five or six months during the winter, and everything is provided for you except your food. Linens, towels, cutlery, dishes, etc. are all there.

You can rent simply or expensively. And you can also rent summer resorts.

Check out two or three places. Find out when they are busy and when they are empty. Know who to call, how to call, and what you want to arrange. Then, by having several of these phone numbers handy, you have a place to call when the time is ripe for your exodus.

Of course, you can always have your own place that is stocked and ready for you through the advance use of your own money and time.

The advantage of not owning is that you have mobility and can go to another place without too much financial inconvenience at that time of general trouble.

By not furnishing everything yourself, you pack your bags and boxes or trunk and leave on the nearest train, plane, car, or truck for your next stop.

FACT 86—HAVE A FOOD-STORAGE PLAN, FOR FOOD WILL BE YOUR MOST IMPORTANT ITEM.

Food could be in very short supply in the coming depression due to breakdowns in government services, or an oil embargo, or truck delays and strikes, or a hundred other reasons.

You must think of food *now* and prepare for the troubles that will present themselves when you think of going to the local grocery store for a week's supply.

Your chances of getting home with the load of

groceries may be slim. Gangs know where to hang out and who to watch coming and going. Everyone will be vulnerable, especially elderly people. Don't go alone to buy food, and don't go out without some kind of protection on yourself.

Buy dehydrated milk, cream, eggs, potatoes, corn, peas, etc. It is all available for you in large or small quantities *now*. People who do not prepare today with food storage for what is coming tomorrow are extremely foolish.

Don't wake up one morning to read about it, not having any emergency survival food already in your home.

Check the the list of recommended books and products at the back of this book for aids on where and what to buy.

Bottled water will be necessary for cooking, drinking, and mixing dehydrated food with.

You can also consider freeze-dried foods. The process is different from dehydrated allowing you to buy much in the line of meats.

Happy is the provider of any household who can go to sleep at night in this crazy world and know that there is food stored along with water for an emergency of any kind, whether man-made or natural (as in the case of the recent terrible Italian earthquake, in which thousands died of the earthquake, and then disease spread because of rotting bodies and lack of food for the living).

FACT 87—YOU MAY NEED SPECIAL CLOTHING, MATERIALS, AND OTHER EQUIPMENT IN ORDER TO SURVIVE THE COMING TIME OF DISORDER.

After you and your family have decided that you are going to take off (having already decided on the best area for you, suited to your personalities and requirements), then consider what additional items for survival you may need.

Let's assume that you decided on a snow climate in the north. There are distinctly four seasons, one of which will require some special thinking if you are going to live remotely, perhaps in the mountains of British Columbia or the Sierras in California.

Can you afford a snowmobile for transportation over rough terrain if necessary?

What about a four-wheeler for icy climbing and heavily snow-covered roads?

Consider what you would do if the fuel ran out? Can you cut wood? Do you have a buzz saw? Try experiencing it before using it for emergencies.

Check out sources of wood supply in the area you are going to. Check out food supplies and drugs required for the time you may be there.

Some people have the idea of a mini-ranch with a horse or two, cows, chickens, etc. It might be a great idea to study up on these sources of food and power—how to feed, keep, sustain them, etc.

Study some of these ideas in the many books that are available to you in modern bookstores today. Consider the art of fishing for survival. In Florida you could be sustained for a long time if you know where and when to throw the line.

This is also true of Canada and her many lakes teeming with edible fish.

Such things as wild game, fishing, planting, and buying all have to be studied if you are to survive the future catastrophe.

It can be done safely and properly if you study now.

If you decide you want the tropics, consider the diseases of the warmer weather and the medicinal protection you might want to stock up on in order to live where these maladies abound.

Insect repellents, netting, lightweight clothes, and specialized fishing gear for the area you are going to should be considered.

FACT 88—SPECIALIZED COOKING STUDY MAY BE REQUIRED FOR THE AREA YOU ARE HEADED FOR IN THE EMERGENCY, AS WELL AS SPECIALIZED STUDY IN WHAT YOU MIGHT ENCOUNTER THERE.

When you know where you are going, study every book you can find on the terrain, topography, nature, animals, and food provisions that the area affords.

This can be fun and extremely rewarding when the time comes to utilize your newfound knowledge.

For example, if you are planning to go to the islands of the Pacific, do you know how to cook the food that is native to the area? Why not consider learning about it now?

Fish preparation, pork baking, and fruit recipes of the natives would be among the best educations ever, as you travel to these areas, acquainting yourselves with all of this.

Life could be very different for all your family, but it need not be overly difficult.

By the way, the family that has gold can go anywhere, for it is universally accepted and is instantly interchangeable to any type of commodity or currency.

FACT 89—BE PREPARED FOR PROPER COMMUNICATIONS WITH THE OUTSIDE WORLD.

Many people have written me because of my former books and have told me of where and when they are going when things get bad.

They tell me of their arsenal of weapons for hunting and protection. I have learned a lot about survival in the last two years from my friends who have written with terrific ideas.

One point that was brought out was the necessity of taking battery-powered radios with you in case electricity breaks down in your area of living. You *do* want to know what is going on in the outside world.

You want to know how far away the trouble is, and whether it is getting near to where you are.

You will want to know about war breaking out, diseases, or major outbreaks of violence in certain communities.

Communication is important even if you live remotely and without fear of the outer world.

Check out the kind of radio you are buying to find out how good its reception is, and how long the transistors will last in and out of the radio.

You might also consider a two way, shortwave set for emergency communications.

Anything can happen to you and yours, and in situations like this, if there is no phone or other means of communication nearby, what would you do?

Be prepared.

FACT 90—IT IS A FACT RELATED TO ALL THE COMING MONETARY CALAMITIES THAT CHILDREN CAN GET LOST, NEED ENTERTAINMENT, AND HAVE TO BE SPECIALLY GUIDED WHEN YOU MIGHT BE IN A NEW AREA.

Preparation of your little ones is important. Today your child goes to school, watches television, reads books, and plays with neighbors. But what will he or she do when confronted with a new environment?

Are you prepared for this? Plan entertainment ideas for your chidren. Think in terms of their safety outside if you live in the mountains or near the beach.

"Story time" and "book time" may be the most fascinating moments of the day for them (and you) in the future. But it must be planned for now, with the buying of the items needed, as a result of much forethought.

This is one time a good German shepherd dog or a Siberian husky would be a pal and a marvelous source of protection for your children and yourself.

FACT 91—OVER 98 PERCENT OF THE POPULA- TION OF THE NATION WILL NOT BE READY FOR ANY OF THIS. YOU CAN BE PART OF THE 2 PERCENT THAT WILL BE.

Books are being published quite often now by a variety of authors on how to be prepared for the future calamities, and yet most of the population will be entirely at a loss on how to handle it.

The facts will confront them one day, but they will not have any idea where to go or what to do to escape it all.

Hospitals will fill up, as will psychiatric institutions. Drugs will increase alarmingly and thousands of people will steal for food and drug addiction.

Every opiate known to mankind will be utilized, but only the people with the foresight to engage in proper preparation will make it.

You can be a friend and prepare others too. Why not pass out books that will enable others to understand what is going to happen.

What better gift at various times of the year?

Another idea—sponsor a "survival party."

During this party, whether it is indoors or a

backyard barbeque, have a time when everyone sits down as you explain exactly why you invited them to come.

They may be neighbors, church acquaintances, relatives (the hardest to reach are relatives), or just friends from work, school, or social gatherings.

Explain your points one by one, perhaps even by typing out a sheet, duplicating it, and handing it to everyone with a pencil.

Explain what you believe is going to happen and what you feel would be wise to do now in the light of it all.

Throw open the party for discussion, in an orderly fashion, and write down ideas on how to cope with it all. Who knows what new thoughts will arise?

Prepare others for what might come. Even speak to your minister, rabbi, or priest about it. Would he be willing to sit in? To help set things up? To call in an expert on the subject?

But *do prepare others.* Get as many people involved as you can. But remember never to tell anyone about your gold coins—never!

FACT 92—TIMING IS MOST IMPORTANT. YOU DO NOT WANT TO BE TOO LATE IN BUYING THE THINGS YOU WILL NEED, OR IN LEAVING FOR WHERE YOU FEEL THINGS WILL BE SAFEST FOR YOUR FAMILY.

Therefore, let me devote the last ideas to those things you should be watching for in America (or in the nation).

You could be too late to get the things you need by always promising yourself you are going to have plenty of time to get them.

It is possible to be like the people who are too late to get over the last bridge out before the floodwaters come. They always knew that living close to the bridge gave them an edge on everyone else. But they did not watch the weather changes closely enough, and the rising waters overtook them even though they lived close to safety.

No preparation means catastrophe. Not watching events unfold will bring them when you are poorly prepared.

Keep your eyes open for the following things to take place.

FACT 93—WATCH FOR INTERNATIONAL DUMPING OF THE DOLLAR BY OVERSEAS HOLDERS OF BILLIONS OF DOLLARS.

This will indicate, as you hear it and read about it in the news, that the big boys might know something not reported yet to the American people.

It means that insiders have reported overseas that the dollar is nosediving in value. This could indicate that an overnight depression is heading for the United States, unknown to the sleepy Americans.

International bankers, Arab oil tycoons, governments abroad, and large multinational industrialists have their economic eye open for dropping values of currencies, and the symptoms indicating these things may happen soon. They watch symptoms of failure, as in the case of the creation of too much money in the German failure of 1923. They also know at about what point too much is too much (far better than we do). *They know the breaking point.*

There are over 800 billion dollars in overseas pockets now. Holding these dying dollars in the preliminary hours to a depression would be calamitous for the holders. They know better and will dump billions of them quickly in exchange for other commodities and currencies.

When you hear of a flurry of international excitement over monetary exchanges and realize that overseas powers are dumping millions of U.S. dollars on the international exchange, then you know it is all beginning. There will be no recovery from this massive dumping—only corrections in prices and values in America, called *depression*.

FACT 94—WATCH FOR THE SUDDEN JUMP IN THE PRICE OF GOLD INTERNATIONALLY. AS GOLD JUMPS HIGHER AND HIGHER, YOU WILL KNOW THAT INVESTMENTS RELATED TO DOLLAR VALUES HAVE DROPPED AND LARGE AMOUNTS OF INDUSTRIAL MONEY, INVESTMENT MONEY, AND EVEN CENTRAL BANK AND GOVERNMENT MONEY IS GOING INTO THE BEST-KNOWN AND SAFEST HAVEN OF ALL—GOLD.

You had better watch for this barometric monetary change in the financial weather. This one is certain to let you know that trouble is ahead and will arrive shortly.

Gold jumps because of demand for it. Demand for it comes especially when the dollar is weak and dollar-related equities are also weakening.

A large dumping of money on the market or large amounts of money being created could force large amounts of money into gold.

This will create a whirlwind of demand on the stock exchanges of the world and push the price of gold out of sight.

Don't forget that some of the best brains in the world believe that gold will bottom out at about $3,000 per ounce when this day hits. I too believe that this is possible.

When gold values climb in a spectacular fashion over a weeks' time, you should know that something big is happening internationally, and it is related to your dying dollar.

FACT 95—WHEN INTEREST RATES IMPOSED ON THE NATION BY THE MULTINATIONAL BANKS ARE RISING TO 30 PERCENT AND MORE, THEN YOU KNOW WE ARE HEADED FOR A TERRIBLE FALL IN THE NATION.

Even now we are staggering in business all across the nation. But can you imagine the calamities that will befall industry when interest rates get to this all-time high? I'm not sure any of us can imagine the calamities to come to this point.

We could easily see the nation shut down!

Who can afford 25 or 30 percent borrowing? There would be only one organization that would attempt it—the government.

If the government of the United States needs a lot of money at that time (and they will because taxable income will be slipping due to lack of business and jobs), then the government will be buying money with bonds and securities from the Fed with our money to pay it off in years to come, thus increasing the government debt to astronomical amounts.

The money fed into the system of the banking world of the U.S. at that time through government borrowing from the Federal Reserve System will become more and more useless.

Eventually it could reach the point when it will not be worth the paper it is printed on.

When you see interest rates soaring even worse than now, get ready for the future presented in this book.

FACT 96—WHEN YOU HEAR THE GOVERN-MENT SUGGESTING AND/OR DEBATING THE

ISSUANCE OF A NEW PAPER MONETARY SYSTEM FOR THE PEOPLE OF THE UNITED STATES, THEN KNOW WE ARE READYING FOR AN ECONOMIC FALL.

There has been much talk in economic circles that one of the ways out that is available (instead of a depression) would be the creation of a new paper currency backed by the government.

But what will make it any different from what we have now? As long as we have a currency not related to any sensible item (such as gold) to back it, why will it be worth any more than our current system? Only if backed by land values would it work.

But this would only bring about a psychological change of values. It might halt the tide of depression for a few weeks or even months, as it could effectively change the thinking of big business for awhile. But not forever.

However, I am only reminding you and myself that when you hear of this pending, and hear of Congress and the Fed discussing it, know that the end is near.

Take the proper precautionary steps to getting your family into a place of safety if you can.

If you are aging and cannot move (nor are being considered by your children for a move with them), you can let them know how you feel about these things and spur them into action yourself, with you involved.

However, if you are not able in any way to move, consider joining forces with others of your age group (if possible) and share apartments, houses, or condominiums with one another for the time of trouble.

The question is often asked how pension recipients will fare.

It will be very tough for them prior to the depression, as prices will climb due to interest rates and inflation. They will find it much better *during* the depression as they continue to receive their checks from Social Security, etc.

They will find their purchasing power better in a depression than in a period of hyperinflationary costs.

The point is that they must get their checks. Joining forces with others in the same situation and moving temporarily to another, less-inhabited area might even cut costs now.

Smaller areas offer lower costs for apartments, services, and goods, as a rule.

FACT 97—WHEN YOU HEAR OF BANK FAILURES IN THE UNITED STATES COMING RATHER RAPIDLY, KNOW THAT WE ARE READYING FOR THE DEPRESSION.

I am not speaking of hundreds of banks, but only of several—perhaps less than a dozen.

When you read of this happening (hopefully they will let us know and not hide the news), then you will want to be ready for further monetary catastrophies soon.

Bank failures come for a variety of reasons, but when they come they hit hard.

Do not count on the FDIC being able to bail out the nation's banks. Only about 1 percent of the total deposits on hand today are actually covered by the FDIC. If a few of the banks go under, the FDIC would be hard-pressed to cover the losses.

The Arab oil nations, with billions of dollars in our banks, could pull them out for exchange with other currencies and thereby precipitate bank failures.

Even sales of U.S. dollars for other currencies as enacted by overseas investors in this nation could cause bank failures.

If all of OPEC decided suddenly not to accept U.S. dollars as payment for oil products any longer, we could be in terrible jeopardy in the banking world.

If the Fed calls in the loans it has to member banks, and the member (local) banks have to call in their loans from the businesses of the community, then you know we are in for a quick fall.

There are several good newsletter services, such as my own Doug Clark Survival Letter and others, that will alert you to what is happening in these areas.

Think about subscribing to several newsletters if you can. They each approach the economic, political, and military problems of today differently.

FACT 98—WHEN THE PAPERS AND NEWS MEDIA TELL US THAT ANOTHER AND LARGER-THAN-EVER OIL EMBARGO IS BEING CONSIDERED BY OPEC AGAINST AMERICA, THEN YOU KNOW WE ARE HEADED FOR THE WORST.

I attempted to tell the whole story in my book *The Coming Oil War*. We cannot live without oil in America. We depend on it for a thousand uses and products. Without OPEC oil we would see our industries grind to a halt, and our economy would be in shambles within 30 days of it all happening.

It will hit us with such force as to render the nation numb and senseless.

Unbelievable as it may sound, I believe that we are going to see the day when our oil supply will be cut off and thus produce war. How we are going to run a war without imported oil simply means that there will be rationing of every product known to this nation.

Food will be rationed, energy sources will be rationed, and all industry except military production will be cut back, due to lack of energy and the necesssity of placing what we do have into military preparedness.

How glad you will be that you took on a food-storage plan for your family.

How much happier you will be in those unhappy times when you consider all you have studied in order to be prepared for it when it comes! Your family will love you forever for being prepared.

Oil is black gold to the world, and especially the United States of America.

We could possibly get some from Canada and Mexico, but it is difficult to say how much they will need of their own production at the same time.

One of the problems of living in areas that need air conditioning will be the cutoff of electricity. You had better be able to exist in the heat of the South without air conditioning. Suffering will be great. Look for widespread heart failures.

Energy will have to be channeled into government and military uses in order to regain what we have lost in the embargo.

We will go to war over oil. Be ready for it.

FACT 99—BE PREPARED FOR GOVERNMENTAL ISSUANCE OF THE PRESIDENTIAL POWERS ENACTED BY THE FEDERAL EMERGENCY MANAGEMENT AGENCY. THIS WILL BE "FOR THE GOOD OF THE NATION."

When the President (or Vice President and appointed authorities) take control of the nation through FEMA, then we are in trouble again.

I look for this to happen during the decade of the 80's. It is all in perfect position now.

It is frightening when you think of what can happen overnight and thus place this entire nation on emergency alert.

Food production and distribution would be frozen.

You bank account could be frozen and your savings as well. Are we ready for that? You are if you have some gold coins hidden away!

Our houses would be under the President's control or the committee's control, and they could force "joint living"—communal-type living to save expenses.

Mass movements of large segments of the population can be enacted if necessary.

Communications media would be under direct governmental control.

All services of transportation, communications, and utilities would fall under governmental powers.

Think about what could happen to you and yours under these circumstances.

FACT 100—WATCH FOR CIVIL UNREST, DISOBEDIENCE, AND CRIME TO RISE IN YOUR CITY OVERNIGHT.

This is a major sign that things are breaking out in your city.

This means that it is time for you to be ready to do what you have planned to do.

The fires of California each year burn out of control and consume hundreds of thousands of acres of wonderful timberland, to say nothing of millions of beautiful homes, apartments, and condos.

Once the fires start, they burn uncontrollably until expended or finally put out.

Once the fires of rebellion against government waste, unemployment, inflation, interest rates, and hunger start to burn, they will burn like no other fires in American history.

The roots of civil unrest are in place. The burning embers are on the fire, just waiting to be fanned. Then watch the flames of disgust, distrust, rebellion, and hate burn with a fury not seen in our streets since the Civil War—and that was very civil compared to the uncivility of this coming internal combustion in the United States!

FACT 101—BE READY FOR THE SMOKESCREEN OF LOFTY RHETORIC DECLARING WHAT IS HAPPENING TO BE ONLY A NASTY BUT SOLVABLE PROBLEM: "EVERYTHING IS UNDER CONTROL."

It will come in order to calm you and others and to keep you from panic yourself.

It will come from Washington's best. Even our wisest leaders will have to try to "put the fire out."

But please differentiate between the hyperbole from the banking leaders and the advice from politicians who mean well.

The political leadership will be the closest thing to the truth of the statements coming out of Washington.

They will try to calm us, control us, and guide us to their limited extent.

The lies will come from the banking establishment at that time, telling us they have everything under control, and not to panic at all.

"There will be no need to have runs on the bank—your money is fine and safe." They will say lots more, too.

Some wise men will speak, and to listen to what they are saying will help.

The wisest thing you can do is to be ready for all of this in your heart, your pocketbook, and your family affairs.

FACT 102—KEEP YOUR MIND UNDER CONTROL BY EXERCISING COOL THINKING, PROPER

PLANNING, AND SPIRITUAL DEDICATION OF YOUR LIFE, YOUR FAMILY, AND YOUR ASSETS TO GOD.

This is the time (when it happens) that we have been thinking about and preparing for. It is the time to stay calm, when the rest of your family and friends are upset, irrational, frightened, or even acting psychotic in their behavior patterns.

Your faith is in three facts of indisputable favor.

1. You have made your preparations financially in that you turned as many assets as you could into gold coins.
2. In addition, you have made preparations about what to eat, where to go, and how to live should you lose your job and have to leave your home for safer quarters. The plans were well prepared, and now you are ready for the inevitable.
3. You have prayed and placed your faith in God, and you know that He will lead you and direct your footsteps into His will for your all.

You can read and quote the 23rd Psalm as your very own. Read the 90th and 91st Psalm as well. They bring God's power and his wonderful blessings into your life at special times of peril to you and yours.

Now you are ready for all these catastrophes.

It is not the end of the road, but a bend in your road of life.

It is another opportunity to show ingenuity, kindness, compassion, strength, and leadership.

You will come out on top.

If the trial of your faith is more precious than gold that perishes, then we will be more spiritual, and more dedicated than ever to God during these times that are coming. A great professor once said,

"Anything that makes us pray and lean on God is good for us!"

I trust that this book has enabled you to see how the events of our nation parallel the prophecies of the Bible, and that they are being fulfilled *now*. "It is better to trust the Lord than to put confidence in men" (Psalm 118:8 TLB).

For your edification and instruction in biblical prophecy, I suggest that you read the following verses and the books on the opposite page.

1. With reference to World War III, Ezekiel 38,39; Daniel 11:40-45; Revelation 6.

2. With reference to coming economic and political disruption in the world—Matthew 24; Luke 21.

3. Any of the specialized materials listed in the coupon on page 176.

Recommended Reading

CRISIS INVESTING, by Douglas R. Casey
76 Press, P.O. Box 2686
Seal Beach, California 90740

THE WAR ON GOLD, by Anthony C. Sutton
International Self Counsel Press, Ltd.
306 West 25th Street
North Vancouver, British Columbia
Canada

AFTER THE CRASH, by Geoffry F. Abert, Ph.D.
Signet Books
1633 Broadway, N.Y. New York 10019

THE FEDERAL RESERVE AND OUR MANIPULATED
DOLLAR, by Martin A. Larson
Devin-Adair Press
Old Greenwich, Connecticut

RUNAWAY INFLATION, by Jerome F. Smith
Self Counsel Press, Ltd.
306 West 25th Street
North Vancouver, British Columbia
Canada

NONE DARE CALL IT CONSPIRACY, by Gary Allen
76 Press
P.O. Box 2686
Seal Beach, California 90740

RESTORING THE AMERICAN DREAM, by Robert Ringer
Fawcett Crest, New York

A PRIMER ON MONEY, Subcommittee on Domestic
Finance
Committee on Banking and Currency
House of Representatives
88th Congress
U.S. Government Printing Office
by Congressman Wright Patman

DEAR DOUG: PLEASE SEND ME THE FOLLOWING INFORMATION—

☐ 1. *DOUG CLARK SURVIVAL LETTER*. Read by thousands on how to survive the coming catastrophes in America and around the world financially. Many have become very secure following Doug's financial advice for the future.

☐ 2. *DOUG CLARK'S LIST OF BOOKS ON PROPHECY AND ECONOMICS*. Having written for over 20 years, Dr. Doug Clark has many up-to-the-minute reports to send you regarding world situations fitting into biblical prophecy and your world today.

☐ 3. *DOUG CLARK'S LIST OF CASSETTES* on world situations, Bible prophecy, relating current events to your personal situation.

☐ 4. Information on buying gold and silver for survival.

☐ 5. Information on survival food for emergency purposes.

CHECK ANY OR ALL FOR FREE INFORMATION
Write to: Dr. Doug Clark, P.O. Box 11387,
Ft. Lauderdale, FLA. 33339.
